Taking Flight For Girls Going Places

Taking Flight For Girls Going Places

A PREVENTIVE TOOL TO HELP KEEP INDEPENDENCE-BOUND GIRLS SAFE, EMPOWERED, AND FREE

• • •

Kathy Greene Lahey

ISBN: 1979648832
ISBN 13: 9781979648837
Library of Congress Control Number: 2017917575
CreateSpace Independent Publishing Platform
North Charleston, South Carolina

Contents

Disclaimer

• • •

THE PURPOSE OF THIS BOOK is to offer material that can aid in self-empowerment and self-protection. The reader acknowledges the inherent risks involved with self-defense as well as the fact that there are no guarantees of safety. You agree that in no way does the author or Presence To My Self, Ltd., assume responsibility for any injuries, harm, or damage that may result from reading this manual. You also accept responsibility for your overall physical and mental fitness, and you acknowledge that you have consulted your physician before engaging in these activities.

A Note

• • •

No BOOK ON SELF-PROTECTION IS complete without calling attention to the offender—the bully, the catcaller, the stalker, the peeping tom, the harasser, the thief, the controlling boyfriend, the cyberbully, the domestic abuser, the kidnapper, the rapist, or the murderer—the people who choose to inflict their harmful agenda on an innocent person.

To be clear, not all offenders are male, and not all victims are female. But in the case of violence toward girls and women, it is usually a male offender. So in this book, we will speak in those terms, knowing that offenders can also be female and that victims can also be male.

It is unfortunate that most females will experience at least one act of violence in their lifetimes. It is unfortunate that we live in a culture, in a world, where violence against females is so epidemic that it is the norm. It is unfortunate that we live in a world where offenders have the need or desire to hurt others.

Perhaps this will change when boys are taught to respect girls and women and to find alternative ways of coping and relating—or maybe when we, as a culture, stop objectifying females. Perhaps this will change when we create laws that ensure females equal power physically and financially or laws that really effect change in the behaviors of offenders. This issue of violence against females—this reality—is deep and complicated, as are the solutions. In the meantime, we need this book on self-protection. It is unfortunate, but we do.

I would like to commend all the individuals and organizations that bring awareness and solutions to the issues of violence, inequity, and safety, including Eve Ensler's V-Day Movement and One Billion Rising Campaign; the #MeToo and #NeverAgain movements; Everytown For Gun Safety and and Moms Demand Action; NOMORE.org; and the Rape, Abuse, and Incest National Network (RAINN). The list is long and the problem multifaceted. May we all do our piece to end injustice and violence around our world.

And I especially want to raise up all survivors of any abuse; may you find your courage, your voice, and your healing.

The Personal Bill of Rights

• • •

I have the right to
be treated with respect.

I have the right to
express my opinion.

I have the right to
show my feelings.

I have the right to
feel safe.

I have the right to
have other friends and
outside interests.

I have the right to
privacy and time alone.

I have the right to
say no.

Kathy Greene Lahey

I have the right to
start a relationship slowly.

I have the right to
be myself.

I have the right to
spend time with my own friends.

I have the right to
tell my partner that
violence will not be tolerated.

I have the right to
end a relationship.

—SOURCE UNKNOWN

My Story

• • •

TAKING FLIGHT FOR GIRLS GOING Places was inspired by a life of deep insecurities and lack of personal power, and it blossomed with a decision to take responsibility for my future. As a young girl with poor self-esteem and very little confidence, I went to great lengths to feel that I fit in—that I mattered. Nothing was more important than to be accepted by those around me. Unfortunately, as my independence grew, this hunger would turn into the perfect recipe for victimhood, as though I had the words "Pick me, bad guys!" written across my forehead.

As a teen, I ran across many harmful people and situations that were just *waiting* for girls like me who could easily be manipulated, controlled, and hurt. By the time my midtwenties rolled around, my journey included a peeping tom, stalking, thefts, and many sexual assaults, including rape. Lacking a sense of personal value or any basic safety skills, I put myself in very dangerous situations, and honestly, I am lucky to be alive.

Finally, at age twenty-four, broken and alone, I was at the bottom. Life as a victim was no longer bearable, and something needed to change. It was time to take full responsibility for my life, or I was in for a serious catastrophe—not that I hadn't already suffered enough. With great determination, I picked myself up, found healthy support, and began to practice self-care and healthy decision making.

It was with a deep determination to live fully, safely, and freely that I found new tools for living that became my guides, and I actively applied them every day. By embracing my power and my courage, I became more able to respond to life with confidence and a newfound enthusiasm. Throughout this book, I share several true experiences from my life in which I was a victim or potential victim. It is my hope that in sharing this with you, my suffering will serve to develop your peace and safety as you too incorporate healthy tools into your daily living.

In truth,
Kathy Greene Lahey

CHAPTER 1

Heading Out!

• • •

YAY, YOU'RE GROWING UP! AFTER years of hanging with Mom, Dad, big sister or brother, and, yes, *the babysitter*, you have come to that time in your life when you can strike out on your own and walk toward total independence.

Before you know it, you'll be making your own rules, answering to no one but yourself. Think about it: tacos for breakfast and Pop-Tarts for dinner (or whatever suits you). No more bed making or dish washing (unless you choose to). And curfew? Ha! That. Is. In. The. Past! It's so exciting you can hardly stand it, right?

Whether you have just turned the corner into adolescence or you're about to go off to college, growing up means you will have fewer restrictions, less supervision, and more opportunities for self-care. It is a time to make decisions about your health, relationships, education, and career and to create a journey forward that is all that you dream it to be. *Taking Flight For Girls Going Places* is written to help guide you through *all* the opportunities and challenges that may greet you along the way.

Girls are given hair and makeup tips. They learn about algebra, eating disorders, and hip-hop dancing. They can spot the newest gadget from a mile away. But what do they know about personal safety?

Ask youself this:

When Mom or Dad stops protecting you 24-7, how will you keep yourself safe?

Young children are taught simple safety guidelines and skills that help to keep them safe: Never get into a stranger's car. Don't tell anyone that you're home alone. Use the buddy system at the park, playground, or public restroom. These basic safety tips are taught early in life, but they continue to be important well into adulthood.

The problem is that too often in early adolescence, we stop talking about these lifesaving skills, and they are forgotten. So just as you begin to experience new situations and meet new people on your own, the safety dialogue stops, while the risk increases. It is vital that girls *continue to learn, know, and practice* personal-safety ideas and strategies. They need to apply this knowledge to their current life situations and be *prepared* to move forward safely.

Education is your best defense!

While most people are good, decent people, there are those who do not have your best interests at heart. Some people mean you harm, and unfortunately, bad things do happen. Women (and men) are violated in various ways every day, everywhere. The good news is that even though there are many dangers out there, there are also simple, practical ways to lessen your risk and often prevent such situations from happening to you.

As you educate yourself with the information in *Taking Flight For Girls Going Places*, you will begin to think of your safety more often and to act in a safer manner. You will learn how to recognize and avoid dangers when possible and how to become more able to respond to various harmful people and situations.

CHAPTER 2
Why This Book?

• • •

As CHILDREN WE LEARN IMPORTANT information about fire safety and stranger danger. We are told not to play with matches, to lock the doors when home alone, and to never ever get in a car with a stranger. But then what? What safety guidelines are given to us as we become increasingly independent? How will we know if a person or a place actually is unsafe? And how are we to respond to an actual situation in which we *do* have to defend our life?

Many of us live in fairly safe environments, free from worry or threats of danger. But, likewise, we don't live in bubbles. We travel to school, the mall, the ATM, concerts, and the workplace. We go for walks in the city, runs in the park, and rides on the bus or in a taxi. And, especially during the teen years, it's all about meeting new people and encountering new situations and opportunities.

As we see in the daily headlines, danger strikes every corner of our neighborhoods, our country, and our world. In fact, most days, *several* headlines detail incidents of violence, especially violence against females. Whether you are at home, in a car, on the street, at school or the workplace, on campus, at the ATM, or running through the park, there are many dangers waiting that can and will change your life for the worse. It is imperative that you learn what you can do to decrease your risk of these dangers and to be safe wherever you go.

Violence against females is a serious problem. According to the World Health Organization (2013), an estimated 35 percent of women worldwide have experienced either physical or sexual intimate-partner violence or sexual violence by a nonpartner at some point in their lives, with some national estimates going up to 70 percent! To give you a clear picture of this reality, below is a list of statistics, and they are staggering. We all may know that violence against females is widespread, but to see the actual numbers is just that: staggering.

DID YOU KNOW THESE FACTS?

* Among high-school students who dated, 21 percent of females experienced physical or sexual dating violence (Vagi et al. 2015).
* There were 431,840 victims (age twelve or older) of rape and sexual assault in 2015 in the United States (Truman and Morgan 2015).
* Sexual assault, including rape, occurs most commonly among women in late adolescence and early adulthood, usually in the context of a date (Abbey 2002).
* Almost two-thirds of all rapes are committed by someone who is known to the victim. Seventy-three percent of sexual assaults were perpetrated by a nonstranger: 48 percent of perpetrators were a friend or acquaintance of the victim, 17 percent were an intimate, and 8 percent were a relative *(Bureau of Justice Statistics 2010).*
* In one survey, approximately 10 percent of female high-school students reported having been raped (Grunbaum et al. 2002).
* One out of six American women has been the victim of attempted or completed rape in her lifetime (National Institute of Justice and Centers for Disease Control and Prevention 2015).
* When sexual assault occurred, 48 percent of victims were sleeping or performing another activity at home; 29 percent were traveling

to and from work or school or traveling to shop or run errands; 12 percent were working; 7 percent were attending school; and 5 percent were doing an unknown or other activity (Bureau of Justice Statistics 2013).

Why We Need This Book

- Raise awareness of the extent of violence against females.
- Become aware of the various dangers we could face.
- Teach us how to become more alert, cautious, and safe.
- Prevent/minimize these acts of violence.
- Help us live in the solution rather than be part of the problem.
- Help us build happy and healthy relationships.
- Build self-esteem and self-empowerment.

There is a solution. For most of the threats we face in our lifetime, there are safeguards. These are simple measures or strategies that we can take to avoid or minimize the chance of being involved in certain dangers. Remember, if we don't play with matches, we will not start a fire. In a similar way, you can reduce your chance of being a victim of a crime. Simply knowing how an offender chooses his (or her) victims will help you avoid being chosen. For example, by eliminating the advantage of surprise gained by a potential offender, you can avoid being a victim. Pay attention! That is one simple safeguard against potential danger.

Now, the victim is never at fault. Nobody would choose to be bullied, stalked, assaulted, raped, or killed. That doesn't mean you should not do whatever you can to avoid putting yourself in potentially dangerous situations. Although there is no guarantee of safety, you certainly can try your best to take necessary and available precautions.

From using your mind to using your body, the various self-protection tools are within your capabilities.

So how can you prevent yourself from becoming a victim? You are more capable than you think. From using your mind to using your body, you have various self-protection tools. Who can't learn to walk in heavily lit and populated areas or to avoid high-risk activities like hitchhiking? Who can't discover the vulnerable areas of the body that will succumb to a good pinch, hit, or kick? And who doesn't have an inner voice that nags her when something is wrong?

Empowering yourself with the information in *Taking Flight For Girls Going Places* will often mean reinforcing what you already know. And that is important. Some of the information may be new, and you may need to read it a few times before you really absorb it. While reading, it is important to put yourself in the different scenarios and imagine how you would respond in the most appropriate, safest manner. Continue to *think safety* as you walk through your day, and then practice, practice, practice so that it becomes second nature! It is easier to prevent a situation than to have to fight for your life!

Spread the Word

This information can make a huge difference, one life at a time, starting with you. Read the pages, imagine yourself responding in a powerful way, implement the preventive guidelines, and practice the moves. Share this message of empowerment with your friends, including the males in your life. Tell them what it is like to simply walk down the street and be catcalled and treated like a sexual object. Tell them how the threat of rape and stalking affects your everyday life. Ask them to speak up when they hear of attitudes and behaviors that degrade females. The more males understand the impact of these experiences, the higher the chance these behaviors will end.

SPEAK UP!

Don't be afraid to report crimes that happen around you, in your home, in your neighborhood, or on your campus. If you are the victim of a crime, go to the authorities, and exercise your rights. By reporting these crimes, you may prevent someone else from suffering at the hands of your offender. This important step will allow you to process the trauma and begin to heal. And who knows, it may even help the offender understand the effects of his actions and lead him to change.

Violence against girls and women is not a female issue. As daughters, sisters, mothers, girlfriends, wives, and grandmothers are made victims, fear and hopelessness spread across families and communities. Let us all work together to empower ourselves and get the message out there that we will not sit quietly and allow these statistics to continue or worsen.

We must do whatever is in our power to prevent ourselves from becoming victims. And we must publicly speak out against the many societal messages that portray females as inferior, which leads to a society of powerless, voiceless victims. It starts with you.

Violence against girls and women is not a female issue. As daughters, sisters, mothers, girlfriends, wives, and grandmothers are made victims, fear and hopelessness spreads across families and communities.

ABOVE AND BEYOND

1. List three safety precautions that have helped keep you safe through your lifetime.
2. Talk to a male relative or friend about violence against females. Tell him how this reality affects your life.

CHAPTER 3

Living in Safety

• • •

Dɪᴅ ʏᴏᴜ ɢʀᴏw ᴜᴘ ɪɴ a *safe* environment, one where the chance of becoming a victim of a crime seemed unimaginable? Perhaps you heard about a mugging, a rape, or even a murder, but it happened to somebody else, far away from your home. On the other hand, maybe violence was a part of your everyday life, and you grew up feeling vulnerable and on guard. This scenario is unfortunately quite common. Whatever your situation, most girls are aware that our world is not always a safe haven without risk or danger.

Independence happens over time. It starts when you are a young child and you learn to choose how to dress in the morning.

Whether you had caring adults protect you as a child or not, growing up can be a frightening experience. Even if you are familiar with conflict or violence, it does not mean you are best prepared to deal with it—that you have learned to avoid it or confront it and to protect yourself. You need to know and apply appropriate, effective safety skills that are available to you.

Luckily, independence doesn't happen overnight. Children usually don't go from complete dependence on their parents one day to being left on their own the next. No, independence happens over time. It starts when you are a young child and you learn to make simple decisions about the details in your life. Remember picking the colors to use in your drawing or the clothes you wanted to wear to school? How about choosing which extracurricular activities to join? Ask yourself these questions:

- As a child, did you have absolute control over your decisions, or were they made with the help of an adult?
- Did the potential outcome of each decision dictate how much power you had in the decision making?
- If there was more risk involved, was there more adult guidance?

Probably the choice of colors to use in a picture was all yours, since little danger can come from deciding to draw a green elephant! However, wearing clothes that are unsuitable for the weather may have more serious consequences, so the adults around you might have been more involved. How about your curfew or driving privileges? How were those decisions made?

Simple, low-risk decisions can help children gradually embrace their sense of personal power and responsibility. Through making simple decisions about the colors or clothing they prefer and then living with the consequences of these decisions, children learn how their choices affect them and the world around them. They learn to have a sense of control over their lives. They learn that they have the ability to respond in an appropriate, sensible way. And in time they will learn about the freedom to be who they are—not who others want them to be.

DO YOU TRUST YOURSELF TO MAKE APPROPRIATE, SENSIBLE DECISIONS?

The teen years are especially loaded with opportunities to develop decision-making skills. As your world expands and you embrace new relationships, activities, and ideas, you get to discover who you are. You get to see what makes you feel good and what makes you feel right, and you get to choose who and what you want in your life. As you make appropriate, healthy choices, you create the life that you want for yourself, and eventually, you fly on your own. It is your life, after all.

No problem, right? Sure! Most teens would agree that growing toward independence is exciting. But *easy*? Probably not. Like that young girl challenged with an empty page and a big box of crayons, the adolescent has so many choices and decisions, and each decision affects the next, which then affects the next, and so on. It can be confusing, overwhelming, quite messy—and not so simple. So how to cope? In a world charged with tremendous opportunity *and* risk, you cope by trying and hoping for the best but preparing for the worst.

In a world charged with tremendous opportunity and risk, you cope by hoping and trying for the best but preparing for the worst.

Some of the challenges teens face include school, family, friends, sports, clubs, jobs, and religious activities. Add to that a changing body, overly enthusiastic hormones, and a social landscape even Columbus couldn't navigate. Sounds like a recipe for modern-day mayhem, right? But even with all that activity, most teens trudge through their adolescent journey with few major complications—definitely many stressors, but few major snags!

Unfortunately, though, the one stressor that can undermine everything else—the one element of reality that can affect even the most routine affairs—is your safety. Think about it. How are you supposed to do well in school, go for a run, or relax at the mall when you feel you are at risk? Even if you are not in actual danger, the belief that you *could* be in danger robs you of your confidence in the world. Lack of security can limit your ability to explore, meet new opportunities, and live to your fullest potential. Consider how stressful it is to just *think* danger could be lurking around any corner, especially a danger for which you are unprepared.

Now, do teen girls feel at risk? Do you feel at risk? What dangers do you perceive in your world? Were you aware of the probability of facing the dangers outlined in this book? Do you believe they can happen to you? According to an article in *Psychology Today* on teen vulnerability and risk, studies have shown that changes in the brain during early adolescence make teens more focused on the rewards of peers and being included in peer activities. This increased focus on peers occurs during a time when other portions of the brain are not yet ready to assist in mature self-regulation, resulting in a perfect storm of opportunities for risky behavior (Magliano 2015). So, while the primary focus is peer relations and acceptance, teens often miss the actual dangers around them, and they don't have the natural capability to deal with what may come. But, importantly, they can learn.

The reality is that violence against females can and does happen everywhere. It happens in every town and in every school, and it affects every age and socioeconomic group. It even happens to people who take every precaution they know of. Yes, random acts of violence do happen.

As you grow up, you learn how to navigate the world at large so your dreams and goals can be realized. And since violence is a reality in our world, one of the best decisions you can make is to prepare for the dangers that you may face. By acknowledging and preparing for danger, you actually can live with more confidence and security because you know you have what it takes to protect yourself to the best of your ability.

How many times have you been told to "be nice"? Don't yell, don't pinch, don't hit, don't bite, don't spit, don't throw rocks, don't curse, don't kick, don't fight.

Nice girls don't always win. One of the ironies of growing up in an unsafe world is that females are conditioned to be nice, caring, sweet, sensitive, and polite. They are rewarded for charitable characteristics and punished for showing any signs of power or aggression. How many times have you been told to "be nice"? Don't yell, don't pinch, don't hit, don't bite, don't spit, don't throw rocks, don't curse, don't kick, don't fight. Such behaviors would never be tolerated at home or school, and they would in fact get you in a lot of trouble. So we become good girls, "nice girls," and we keep our voices down and our hands by our sides. If we get the urge to stand up for ourselves, we stuff it and often end up directing that anger inward.

Well, what do we do when someone crosses our boundaries? What about when we are spoken to in inappropriate or disrespectful ways? What about when we are touched without our permission? How are we supposed to speak up in the face of danger when our voices have been silenced or at least muffled?

It is shocking how females are taught as young girls to become victims.

Wake up! Raise your left hand high in the air. Now, with your right hand, grab the underside of your left arm, right under your bicep—that skin that hangs down a bit. Now pinch yourself there. Go ahead—pinch hard. It hurts, right? Not very nice, huh? Good. Consider that your wake-up call. Sometimes in life we need to send a message loud and clear. And sometimes nice, kind words don't do the job. Sometimes we need to step up the heat a little and let someone know we mean business. *So do we have your attention?*

Every day we view news headlines of females who have been hurt: mugged, stalked, kidnapped, sexually assaulted, raped, or murdered. Frankly, we are bombarded with these stories. In looking deeper into these accounts, you will notice that some of these acts of violence were unpreventable, and they were certainly not the victims' fault. On the other hand, many of them *could have been prevented* if females were taught some basic self-protective, self-empowerment skills.

You are not a helpless victim. You have a voice. Declare your right to a safe and respectful environment. Things must change. We as females need to *make the decision and commitment* to teach people how to and how *not* to treat us!

Females are not helpless victims. Girls and women have a voice to declare their right to a safe and respectful environment.

HONOR YOUR LIFE

This book is about honoring your life as the gift that it is. It is about taking ownership of your safety, your sense of responsibility, and your self-esteem. Just the fact that you are choosing to educate yourself with the information in *Taking Flight For Girls Going Places* says that you are ready to take charge of your life.

Hopefully the pinch woke you up to realize you need to do a little work to keep yourself safe. (And it's a great defensive move. Even a three-year-old can do it!) After embracing the information in this book, you will know how to minimize your chances of becoming a victim, and you will possess the ability to defend yourself should the need arise. Although little in life is absolutely certain, empowering yourself with this material can help you to move through your days with more safety, confidence, and freedom.

Each day, be sure to listen to your inner voice for the direction and guidance you will need. Stay open and true to yourself. Resist all pressure to be someone you are not. If you ever feel discomfort or unease in *any* situation, with *any* person, you have the right and ability to leave. You have the right to take care of yourself first, whatever that may mean.

You are a unique piece of the divine. Be in your peace! Be your divine self! As you move out from your corner of the world and grow into all you are meant to be, live this truth. Do what is right for you. In doing so, you will help to create a more truth-filled, peace-filled, divine-filled world.

ABOVE AND BEYOND

1. What three decisions have you made in your life that helped you feel more competent?
2. How close have you been to any act(s) of violence? Describe your feelings about the experience.
3. What does it mean to be your divine self? Your true self?

CHAPTER 4

Prevention

• • •

My friend rented a basement apartment in the home of a couple with three young daughters. One day, the mom took the girls out of town, leaving her husband—who was a police officer—home. My friend ran into the husband in their driveway, where he invited her for a drink later that day. Since she knew the family and had never had a problem, she accepted.

Early in their visit, the man approached my friend in a sexual manner. He continued to try to get his way, against her wishes, eventually cornering her up against a wall. Luckily, she fought back and was able to escape, but not without a struggle.

That night, I received a desperate call from her. Within a few hours, several of us had her packed and moved out.

Although we tried to convince her to report the incident to the police, she refused. She just wanted to get out and be safe. A few months later, this husband, father, and police officer was arrested, convicted, and imprisoned for raping a different woman.

• • •

WHO IN THE WORLD WOULD want to be involved in a robbery, assault, or attack? Most people would choose peace and security over any kind of conflict. So how can you maintain a level of well-being in a world that has, in fact, much risk? How can you get through each day without having to use self-defense? You prevent it from happening in the first place.

Prevention is your greatest defense.

There are several methods that criminals use to approach their victims. Depending on what an offender is looking to accomplish, he will choose different approaches. He may lie to attract your attention and then move on from there; for example, a man may pull over in a car to ask you for directions, but really he wants to show you his privates. A date may pressure you to move beyond boundaries you choose for yourself. An offender may choose to surprise you when you least expect it—like on that hidden path you take to school—and he may attack you when you least expect it. Many factors can determine how an offender chooses his approach. Personal preference is one, but others can be determined by timing and opportunity. Lots of factors, right?

How can you possibly protect yourself when there are so many unknowns? You need to prepare for *all* of these possibilities. Expect it! Expect the man in the car to be an exhibitionist. Expect someone hiding behind the tree on that hidden path on your way to school. Expect to be ambushed when you are by yourself in an isolated area. Expect it and avoid it.

If you think the man in the car may be up to no good, how can you avoid becoming his victim? For one, don't go near his car. You can walk in the opposite direction, and if he follows you, run to safety, and report it to an adult. How can you avoid becoming the victim of the man on the hidden path? Don't be there alone, don't be there in the dark, or better yet, don't use that hidden path at all! Walk to and from school in well-lit, populated areas, or get a ride. Simple, right? Expect danger, assess the situation for risk, and act accordingly.

You will begin to see each tidbit of information
in this book as a potential lifesaver.

It may seem like a lot of worry and suspicion, but when you become aware of the many dangers in your world, you will begin to see each tidbit of information in this book as a potential lifesaver. At the least, it can be a simple way to prevent an unfortunate situation—a situation that you may never even know you avoided because you were busy living your life safely and freely! And frankly, it is always better to be safe than sorry. It's that simple.

The following pages offer simple guidelines to keep you out of danger. Some of these ideas may seem like common sense—probably because they are. But even so, many are ideas that need to be dredged up, reinforced, or even learned for the very first time. Regardless, it is important to embrace this information and put it into action until these skills become a natural way of living and responding to your world. Although there is no guarantee of safety, these guidelines will make a difference. Again, you may never know the dangers you avoided by putting these principles into your life, but you will know a stronger, safer, and more confident you!

Basic Principles of Safety

* Always trust your instincts or gut. If you feel like something is wrong, it probably is. Pay attention to that feeling!
* Always be aware of who is around you. Is someone watching you or following you?
* Be aware of your environment; understand your surroundings.
* Expand your vision to at least twenty to thirty feet around you. Always know the emergency (escape) exits. Use your environment to your advantage.

- Use all your senses, especially your ears and eyes.
- Do not look like a victim. Walk with self-respect and confidence. Show that you are aware and in control and that you know where you're going.
- If you appear as a victim, you could affirm an attacker's choice of you as a victim!
- Assailants want privacy, control, and the ability to surprise you. Avoid situations that could provide these conditions.
- Fight versus flight? If you are able, always take flight. Do not fight if you have the chance to safely leave a dangerous situation.
- Leave *any* uncomfortable or dangerous situation immediately.
- Program your cell phone with emergency numbers (parents, police, etc.).
- Never allow someone to take you to a secondary crime scene where an assailant has the privacy to do what he chooses. Drop to the ground and make a scene if you are being forced into isolation.
- Alcohol and drugs will affect your judgment and ability to recognize potentially dangerous situations. They will weaken your ability to fight back if necessary.

Your instincts are a gift. In relating with people, the importance of trusting your gut instincts cannot be stressed enough. This doesn't mean that people are generally *bad* and you need to be on guard. It's great to be open to others, because you never know who will cross your path. However, when you are present in the moment and in touch with your instincts, you are in touch with important information you just may need in the face of a threat or danger.

Notice how you feel when you are with someone who is really happy. Now notice how you feel when you are around someone who is angry. What are your physical and mental responses or reactions to each situation? What are the differences? Can you see how your gut offers you advice and protection in the face of conflict? Do you ever feel like something is "not right," but you can't quite put a finger on it? Well, learn to *trust that*!

ABOVE AND BEYOND

1. Which basic principles of safety do you already practice in your life?
2. Which three principles of safety will you implement in your life this week? Continue to add these to your life until you practice them all.
3. Describe an instance when your instincts gave you information. Did you listen? What followed?

CHAPTER 5

Alcohol and Drugs

● ● ●

I was suicidal. My life felt hopeless. Everything felt wrong, and it seemed that no matter what I did, nothing changed. People constantly let me down; I let myself down. I became so afraid of failing that I stopped trying. I thought I was a failure.

Alcohol and drugs took all of that away. When I was high, everything seemed okay—no fear, no cares. It was the solution I was searching for. I didn't realize this "solution" created more problems. My loss of inhibitions and judgment led to nightmares I never imagined, because a drunk girl cannot take care of herself in dangerous predicaments. Eventually, I could no longer look in the mirror without wanting to die.

One morning, I'd had enough. The connection between my "solution"—alcohol and drugs—and my misery became obvious, and I reached out for help. I now have other solutions to life's difficulties. By seeing my own limitations and having the courage and support to change, I am now able to be all I am meant to be.

● ● ●

THIS BOOK IS ABOUT TAKING responsibility for your life. After all, it is *your life* to do with as you choose—in relationships, education, career, hobbies, and health. You will face many tough decisions, decisions that can alter the course of your life for good. One of those decisions is whether to drink alcohol or use drugs.

Using a substance involves risk. Aside from the legal aspects, like underage drinking and using drugs that are illegal or not prescribed by a doctor, there are many factors to consider before you decide to use any substance. Realistically, some people will use these substances without any recurring problems, and others will not. But many teens who decide to use substances face serious consequences early on, and they begin to lose control over their lives.

Drinking alcohol or using drugs can greatly impair your ability to care for and protect yourself. Take great caution when you make these decisions. Think about the consequences. Ask yourself, Is it worth it? Use precautions. When you consume substances, one of the first things affected is your judgment, which alters your perception. One drink or one nonprescribed pill can change your thoughts, your decisions, and your life.

Adding alcohol and drugs to the mix only increases the chance for trouble, and even a fun, innocent time can easily turn into a nightmare. Be aware of your actions, and get help if you need it.

Another risk with alcohol or drugs is losing control over the choice of your use—that is, becoming addicted. Whether someone becomes an alcoholic or addict is determined by several factors, including environment and genetics. Wherever the truth lies, you should know that drinking and drug use run rampant in our society, and there is great risk should you choose to use a substance.

To understand how substance use fits into your life, look at your patterns, and see if you are at risk. What are your attitudes and behaviors with alcohol and drugs, and how do they affect your life? Do your parents or grandparents have a problem with alcohol or drugs? What consequences do you see, in your life or the lives of others around you, as a result of drinking or drug use?

Reports of teen alcohol and drug use are staggering. Deciding whether to join the crowd can be very difficult, especially since drinking alcohol is practically a rite of passage. Here are some things to keep in mind as you make these decisions.

SOME SUBSTANCE-USE STATISTICS

* Underage drinking is a leading contributor to death from injuries, which are the main cause of death for people under age twenty-one. Each year, approximately five thousand persons under the age of twenty-one die from causes related to underage drinking. These deaths include about sixteen hundred homicides and three hundred suicides (National Institute on Alcohol Abuse and Alcoholism 2010).
* At least one-half of all violent crimes involve alcohol consumption by the perpetrator, the victim, or both (Collins and Messerschmidt 1993).

Volumes could be written about this topic, since there are many unknowns in the field of addiction. What we do know is that life is risky enough when you have use of all your senses, and using alcohol and drugs only decreases your ability to keep yourself safe.

SOME CONSEQUENCES OF ALCOHOL AND DRUG USE

* Self-neglect, dishonesty, isolation, infidelity, depression, remorse, and loss of self-respect
* Academic issues such as missed attendance, low grades, and dropping out

* Loss of employment and income
* Illegal possession of drugs and alcohol (if one is underage)
* Relationship issues such as loss of trust, loss of family, and violence
* Gateway substances leading to harder substances
* Car accidents
* Legal issues such as arrests, court appearances, costly legal fees, loss of license, and criminal record
* Medical and physical consequences such as diseases, injuries, overdose, suicide, and death
* High-risk activities (drug dealing, prostitution, burglary, unsafe sexual practices, use of weapons) in high-risk places (bars, drug dens)

ABOVE AND BEYOND

Do you have a problem with alcohol or drugs? The following list is taken from an Alcoholics Anonymous pamphlet. (The author has added the phrase "use drugs.") Try to answer these questions as honestly as possible. If you do have a problem, help is available.

* Do you drink or use drugs because you have problems?
* Do you drink or use drugs to relax?
* Are alcohol or drugs your solution to problems and feelings?
* Do you drink or use drugs when you get mad at others?
* Do you prefer to drink or use drugs alone, rather than with others?
* Are your grades slipping?
* Are you goofing off at work (lateness, absence, stealing)?
* Did you ever try to stop or control (lessen) your drinking or drug use?
* If so, were you successful?
* Do you drink or use drugs in the morning, before school or work?
* Do you gulp your drinks?

* Do you ever have loss of memory due to your drinking or drug use?
* Do you lie about your drinking or drug use?
* Do you ever get into trouble (social, legal, academic, etc.) because of your drinking or drug use?
* Do you get drunk when you drink, even when you don't mean to?
* Do you do things when drinking or using drugs that you would not do when sober?
* Do you think it's cool to be able to hold your liquor or drugs?
* Do you drive after drinking or using drugs?

If you answered yes to any one of these, you need to take a serious look at how your drinking or drug use is affecting you.

CHAPTER 6
Campus, Apartment, and Home Safety

• • •

The sound of footsteps above me was terrifying. Someone was on the roof, watching me through my bedroom window. I couldn't get down the stairs fast enough, where my mother promptly dismissed it as a squirrel. "No way!" I shrieked. I knew what I heard, and that was no squirrel! Outside, no one was in sight, and all was quiet. "Go back inside, and forget about it," I was told. As this happened several times over the next few months, I felt violated, exposed, and vulnerable. I refused to be in my room at night and constantly felt unsafe. The fear of being watched stayed with me for years. Unfortunately, this peeping tom was never caught.

• • •

SAFE AT HOME. WHEREVER YOU call home, it should be a place of comfort and security. This is your space to freely be who you are—the place where you can laugh and love, cry and make mistakes. Whether it's a dorm room, apartment, house, or houseboat, and whether you live on your own, with roommates, or with your family, it's important that you feel safe in every way.

Ideally, you wouldn't have to even think about safety at home. But in reality, many dangers lurk right inside your four walls. When it comes to fire, accidents, theft, and physical assaults, most of these occur in or close to the home. But, as with many dangers, risks at home are often preventable or minimized with the proper response. Living in safety means understanding all the potential dangers and being prepared to prevent or respond to each situation. The following is a list of guidelines to apply to your living situation, whatever that may be.

BOUNDARIES

* Know the police, fire, poison, and student/campus safety emergency-phone numbers. *Do not hesitate to use them.*
* Lock doors, even if you are inside the room, apartment, or home. Use a rubber doorstop to secure from the inside.
* Keep ground-floor and fire-escape doors and windows locked.
* Check to secure any attics, basements, or crawl spaces from outside entry.
* Do not leave personal belongings unattended.
* Do not leave wallets, money, or jewelry exposed on desks or dressers. Keep valuables locked away.
* Engrave your belongings. Photograph your jewelry.
* Record all serial numbers, brand names, and descriptions of valuables. Keep a copy in a separate place. Obtain personal property insurance.
* While gone from your room or apartment, leave a light on, or use a light timer.
* If you live alone, add fictitious names to your mailbox.
* When coming home, have your keys ready before you reach your door.
* Repair or report damaged or defective safety and security hardware.
* Don't leave windows propped open.
* Be sure your address is visible from the street for emergency personnel.

- Use smoke detectors.
- Take fire alarms seriously. Know your exit strategy. If possible, take your keys and leave the building immediately. Upon leaving a smoke-filled building, stay close to the floor. Use the stairs, not elevators. Before leaving a dorm room, feel the door. If it's hot, stay in your room. Open the window, and call for help.
- Fight only small fires—and only after calling 911. Aim the fire extinguisher at the base of the fire, and sweep from side to side. If the extinguisher does not douse the fire, leave immediately, and close the door behind you.
- Always tell someone your plans or schedule, including any changes.
- Avoid working, studying, or being alone in isolated buildings or areas.
- Do not shower in deserted residence hall or gym locker rooms.

Visitors

- Do not provide building access to strangers without keys.
- Do not let strangers in to make a phone call. Take the number, and make the call for them, if you choose.
- Report suspicious people or misconduct to the campus police immediately. Pay attention to details and identification.
- If you encounter a suspicious person inside the stairwell or elevator, leave the building immediately.
- Do not lead a suspicious person to your door. Call the police.
- If you suspect a burglary in progress in your room or home, do not enter. Leave immediately, and call the police.
- Know neighbors whom you could call in emergency.
- Keep a phone near your bed. If you hear a burglar, give no sign of being awake. Call for help only if you can do so safely. Avoid alerting or interrupting a burglar.

- If someone enters your home, leave immediately. If you cannot leave safely, hide. Call the police.
- Never admit workers into your home without proper identification; call to verify their identity and the purpose of their visit.

THE COLLEGE EXPERIENCE

Your years after high school are supposed to be filled with new experiences, self-exploration, and heightened learning. This is a time when you expand your horizons to see what's out there and find your place in it all. In a perfect world, each young woman would be granted the freedom to seek and find, without distraction or interference. Too bad that's not always the case. In fact, for a number of women, the obstacles are many.

Most college dormitories and even off-campus housing have rules and policies put in place to keep students safe. Residence halls have locks to which only residents have access, libraries and student centers require ID cards, and public safety officers are present and available for the needs of the students. Today, there are even more safeguards to promote a safe environment, like mandatory student-safety workshops, proper lighting around the campus, and a staff who is trained to handle various safety issues.

Campus safety programs help to bring greater understanding and awareness to the issues of violence on campus. They send the message that violence against females is campus-wide and that there are specific resources, protocols, and policies in place to prevent or minimize such incidents and to support victims' physical, emotional, and legal well-being.

But even with all these safeguards in place, the college experience can still be dangerous, especially for female students. As statistics show, instances of assault, relationship violence, stalking, sexual assault, rape, and murder are more likely to affect females than males, and college-aged females are more prone to being victimized than any other age group.

A Few Statistics

* During a twelve-month period, an estimated 3.4 million persons age eighteen or older were victims of stalking. Approximately 60 percent do not report victimization to the police (Baum, Catalano, and Rand 2009).
* Persons between the ages of eighteen and twenty-four experience the highest rates of stalking (Baum, Catalano, and Rand 2009).
* Between 1995 and 2013, females ages eighteen to twenty-four had the highest rate of rape and sexual assault victimizations compared to females in all other age groups (Sinozich and Langton 2014).
* In a survey across twenty-seven universities in the United States in 2015, 23 percent of female undergraduate university students reported having experienced sexual assault or sexual misconduct. Rates of reporting to campus officials, law enforcement, or others ranged from 5 to 28 percent, depending on the specific type of behavior (Association of American Universities 2015).
* The National College Women Sexual Victimization Study estimated that between one in four and one in five college women experiences completed or attempted rape during their college years (Fisher, Cullen, and Turner 2000).

Imagine your four best friends. Now imagine which one of you will be raped before you graduate. Why is this population more at risk for victimization? One reason is that most college-aged girls happen to be newly independent and without strong independent-living skills. The level of drug and alcohol use on campuses contributes to the prevalence of crimes and victimization. Couple that with the social, academic, and financial demands, and you will often see highly dysfunctional coping strategies.

It's frightening, right? But do not be dissuaded from going out into the world, studying what you desire, meeting new people, and reaching for your dreams. Just the opposite. Get out there and *be all that you are*! Learn about your environment, and learn about yourself. Become more aware of the dangers so that you can protect yourself from becoming a victim. This information can help you do your best to avoid danger, prevent victimization, and defend yourself if you must. You just have to do the footwork to make that happen.

ABOVE AND BEYOND

1. Which campus, apartment, or home safety guidelines do you already practice in your life?
2. Which three campus, apartment, or home safety guidelines will you implement in your life today? Continue to add these to your life until you practice them all.
3. List the local emergency numbers for the following:
   Public safety:
   Police:
   Crisis hotline:
   Hospitals:
   Fire:

CHAPTER 7

School Safety

• • •

It all started as harmless teasing but it crossed a line. It wasn't the name-calling or the attempt to embarrass me that bothered me so much. After all I gave it right back to him. And we all laughed as though there was no harm done. But there he was. He stood at least a foot above me and weighed maybe twice as much. His presence, grabbing me, cornering me, was intimidating and creepy. And there was something hostile about it, as he pushed his weight and flaunted his power.

Although I laughed it off and held my own in the verbal sparring, I wished he would just leave me alone. I changed my route through the hallways to avoid him, dreaded the classes we shared, and especially hoped the teacher wouldn't have to leave the classroom for any reason leaving me open prey to his harassment.

You would never know how scared I was because I never told anyone. How could I? It was just a joke, right? He never really "hurt" me, right? But I was scared. And it did hurt. And when the teachers shrugged it off as a joke - that made it even worse. My sense of safety and freedom was taken from me, by this boy, and by those who were supposed to protect me.

• • •

YOUR EXPERIENCE AT SCHOOL SHOULD be similar to that at home: a place where you can learn new things, connect with your peers, and grow into who you are meant to be. A place where you can be yourself, free from threat and danger. Besides your home, school is where you will spend most of your time and, ideally, it is where you have trust in your safety.

Although most schools are generally safe places, crises large and small do happen. And, while school safety is a concern no matter ones gender, it is essential you have the tools necessary for safety wherever you are. Incidences of bullying, face-to-face verbal harassment, public humiliation, and physical fighting occur in every school. Both natural disasters (earthquakes, fires, severe weather) and man-made events (bomb threats, active shootings, physical attacks) may also occur. With over 60 million students in schools across the United States, it is necessary to have emergency response plans in place. Just like anywhere else you will travel, you must know how to deal with these situations if and when they occur.

As we will focus more on school emergency preparedness in this chapter, all other safety issues which can also happen in the school are covered throughout this manual.

EMERGENCY PREPAREDNESS

While schools prioritize safety procedures and policies to ensure a positive and secure learning environment for all, they can't always prevent the wide range of events and disasters which could occur. And even though the school's staff has the responsibility to keep you and other students safe, you must take responsibility in maintaining a safe environment wherever you are. In the event of any emergency, along with school officials, you must also participate in these efforts to prevent or minimize threats.

Some of the measures that schools implement to prevent and/or minimize threats include reinforcing a zero-tolerance environment, rules and regulations regarding conduct and dress, anti-bullying trainings, various drills, counseling and conflict resolution programs, the presence of security guards, profiling of potentially violent individuals, and the use of metal detectors. Each school is also connected to local emergency responders, such as the police, fire department, and emergency medical services. And, of course, schools provide an entire staff of professionals available to you, to connect with, talk to, report any incidences, and assure you a safe and successful school experience.

However, even with all of these supports in place, you must do your part. Everyone has a responsibility to create a safe school environment, including students. The following is a list of general safety tips for students:

- Participate in safety planning at school, on the bus, and in the dorms. Practice!
- Follow all safety rules and requests by authorities. They are there to keep you safe.
- Promote an environment that reinforces values of respect, tolerance, empathy, fairness, and personal responsibility.
- Be aware of your environment; use all of your senses (sight, sound, smell).
- Always know the exits wherever you are, and have an escape route and plan in mind.
- Do not provide building access to strangers. Use only those entrances/exits permitted.
- In the case of an emergency, remain calm. Do not panic. Do not let your emotions take control.
- Report any potential problems or suspicious activities to a school official. If a violent situation occurs, notify the nearest school staff

member immediately (teacher, administrator, security personnel, school nurse, guidance counselor, social worker).

* If needed, call 911. Tell them the location of the incident, a physical description of the person(s) involved, type of weapon, if there is one.
* Get out of range of the danger.
* Follow the protocol of an evacuation, lockout, or lockdown.
* Get down low or hide in a room, behind objects, or in a closet. When choosing a location in a room to hide, stay away from the door and choose a location out of sight of the windows
* Prevent individuals from entering any dangerous areas.
* In the absence of adult direction, decide where it is safest to be and remain there until directed.
* During and after the crisis, do not pick anything up, and do not go back for anything until receiving clearance. To the extent that it is safe, keep your belongings with you. Follow direction.

Learning the safety tips in this manual and gaining the knowledge for coping with potentially dangerous situations will help you grow in confidence. Knowing you have the ability to respond to various situations can enhance your sense of safety, as well as actually help you should the fear become a reality. The knowledge you have before an event can offer you a sense of control during a confusing and potentially chaotic situation.

THERE IS NO SINGLE ANSWER.

Each situation is different and these tips can help you assess a situation and apply various options available to you, especially in a time of confusion and fear. To maintain safety and order during an emergency, it is imperative to listen to the direction of authorities, whether it be a school administrator, teacher, security person, or another staff member. Follow what you have learned in your drills and programs designed to deal with these emergencies, including those for evacuation, lockout, and lockdown.

Evacuation: When it is unsafe to stay inside the building, everyone should evacuate to a nearby pre-designated safe location, if possible. This may be an athletic field or alternate building.

- Follow the instructions of school officials or emergency responders.
- When instructed, leave your belongings behind.
- Remain calm.
- Keep your hands visible.
- Help others evacuate, when safe and necessary.
- Move to the designated safe location and remain there until released.
- Do not attempt to move wounded people.

Lockout: During a lockout, access to the building is restricted, but there may be some limited movement within the building. This is used to secure the building from a potential threat outside the building, such as when an unauthorized person is loitering on school grounds or when there is criminal activity in the neighborhood. Follow all instructions of school officials.

Lockdown: In situations involving an intruder or threat of violence in or on a school campus, the building will be locked down with all individuals secured safely inside. Especially if the intruder is inside the building, you will need to:

- Follow the instructions of school officials or emergency responders.
- If you are in a hallway, get into a room and secure the door. Blockade the door with heavy furniture if necessary.
- Move away from doors and windows. Lock them. Close blinds.
- Turn off all lights and other electronic devices. Only use a cell phone if safe to do so.

* Get cover inside a closet or anywhere out of site where the assailant is less likely to find you. Hide behind large items (cabinets, desks).
* Do not open doors or windows unless cleared by school or safety official. Ask for documentation to verify identity of any official.
* Remain quiet; silence your cell phone, turn off any source of noise.
* Dial 911, if possible. If you cannot speak, leave the line open and allow the dispatcher to listen.

AN ACTIVE SHOOTER

It is crucial to prepare for every possible serious threat regardless of its level of probability. School shootings are an unfortunate reality in today's society. This senseless act of violence by another changes the lives of so many forever. Although the chance of an active shooter entering your school may be unlikely, the fear that it could happen is its own crisis. Students who fear for their safety at school are less prone to be fully open to learning and growing.

Over the past 20 years there have been hundreds of school shootings, many which have caused mass fatalities. There have also been mass casualty shootings in other places (church, movie theaters, workplaces, clubs, etc.). In this situation, a person or persons actively engage in killing or attempting to kill people, often at random and usually with the use of a firearm(s). This is an extremely dangerous situation and demands a serious response. You must:

* Remain calm. Do not panic. Do not let your emotions take control.
* Get out of range of the shooter.
* Get down low or hide behind objects or in a closet out of the view of any windows.
* If you are running away, run in a zigzag to make yourself a harder target.

* Prevent individuals from entering an area where the active shooter may be.
* Remain quiet and still.
* Follow the instructions of your teachers, school staff and/or emergency responders.
* In the absence of adult direction, decide where it is safest to be and remain there.
* Follow the protocol of an evacuation, lockout, or lockdown.

Confronting the attacker. Escaping to safety should always be your first priority. A confrontation with an attacker, especially if they have a weapon, should be your last resort. There is a difference between a shooter wanting money or some other material item as opposed to them simply wanting to cause harm. Can you talk or negotiate with the assailant? Can you distract them until help arrives or you can escape to safety? Are you prepared to step it up?

When other options are not immediately possible - complying, hiding, or escaping - your chance of survival is much greater if you attempt to disrupt and/or incapacitate an attacker. As previously mentioned, fighting an assailant is a last resort, but if this is what you decide you must do for survival, here are some critical tips:

* If you have made the decision to attack an assailant, you must commit 100% and give it your all.
* Make a plan. When and how will you strike?
* Know your escape routes at all times. How will you escape once the assailant is disabled?
* Use your environment to your advantage (use furniture, walls to protect yourself).
* Remain calm until the moment you decide to strike.
* At the moment you decide to strike, use your survival scream to increase your power.

* Hit or throw improvised weapons at attackers vulnerable body parts (see chapter 16).
* Follow through until you can escape to safety.

For more information about offense and defense, see chapter 16.

EMERGENCY RESPONSE TEAMS

In the case of any emergency, the police and/or other first responders will respond and attempt to stop the crisis as quickly as possible. It is important to follow their instructions as closely as possible so they can do their job and keep everyone safe, including creating a safe environment for medical assistance brought in to aid any injured.

In the case of an assailant, they will proceed directly to the area in which the last shots or attacks were heard. You must remain calm, put down any items you may be holding and raise your hands in the air so they know you are not the assailant, and proceed to the area they have deemed safe. Stay in that space until you are told you can leave. When it is appropriate, inform law enforcement of any details you have regarding the situation (location and description of the assailant(s), type of weapons, and a report of any injuries at the scene).

AFTER A CRISIS

Any unexpected event can cause fear and concern for all those involved, especially an event which brings with it potential or actual danger. It is important to follow the instructions of those responsible for your safety every step of the way. Schools have in place entire emergency response plans, including your safe return home. There are procedures in place to alert the community at-large, including your parents, about any happenings at school. Just follow their lead and they will walk you through it to the end.

After any traumatic event, it is important to follow up with appropriate support so you can process it and move forward. You may have feelings of sadness, confusion, fear, guilt, anxiety, or anger. You may experience difficulty sleeping, concentrating, or doing your schoolwork. These are normal responses to trauma and you are allowed to move through it as you need. It is important for you take full advantage of the help that is readily available for you to heal and resume your life to the fullest.

Besides the school personnel who are available to help you (teachers, nurse, counselor, social worker) you may also want to connect with your doctor, a therapist, and of course, your parents. Talk with and listen to your classmates, especially if they experienced the trauma as well. This will help each of you walk through it together. You are surrounded by others who are with you on this journey and who will do whatever you need to get through. The emotional, mental, and physical effects of any crisis can be difficult to handle, but you do not have to do it alone.

ABOVE AND BEYOND

1. What safety preparedness drills have you participated in at school?
2. What will you do in the case of an emergency at school? Write down your plans for each potential emergency.
3. What supports are available to process and heal from a traumatic event you may experience?

CHAPTER 8
Street Safety

• • •

I was out at a club one night in an unfamiliar area. Since my friends had already left, taking my ride with them, I decided to hitchhike. Before long, a car stopped, and a man told me to hop in. As he drove, we talked about who knows what until he eventually asked me where I was going. When I told him my home address, he swiftly stopped the car and said that I was going in the wrong direction. After an immediate U-turn, this very decent man stressed how fortunate I was that he was more concerned for my safety than I was, and how easy it would have been for someone else to take advantage of the opportunity I presented them.

• • •

GROWING OLDER ALLOWS YOU MORE freedom to come and go as you please, along with the ability to jump in the car or on a bus or train and go explore new places. Whether you are close to home or in unfamiliar territory, alone or with a group of friends, traveling in public places generates many distinct risks. No matter where you go and how you get there, you will need to follow simple safety precautions so you get there without a hitch (no joke!).

Like all of the guidelines in this book, the following list offers simple but extremely important tips for staying safe in your travels. As you read through the list, imagine yourself walking down the street, practicing each one of these safeguards as it might apply to the situation at hand. Unfortunately, sometimes we forget to use even the most obvious tips, so take your time putting together the words on this page with the actual behavior.

STREET SAFETY GUIDELINES

- *Stay alert!* Focus at least thirty feet away from yourself in all directions.
- If you are uncomfortable with somebody who is coming toward you or near you, *move away* (cross the street, leave the room, or go to a safe place).
- *Do not* go up to a passing car to give directions, help, or other information. If you choose to help someone, keep your distance.
- Avoid shortcuts (isolated trails, alleys, etc.). Plan your route in advance, and always let someone know where you are going. Vary your route and schedule so it is not the same every time.
- *Do not* walk alone at night, especially in unpopulated, unlit areas.
- Travel in groups.
- Walk in an assertive manner. Show that you know where you are going.
- Walk facing the flow of traffic so that you are aware of what is coming at you.
- If a car is following you, turn and run in the opposite direction. Seek a safe place (crowd, traffic, police, school, store, house, etc.) near people and light. Report it to the police. Be aware if a car has passed you more than once.
- Walk in the middle of the sidewalk, away from cars and buildings or alleys where someone could hide and grab for you.
- Do not carry all your money in one place. If robbed, you will not be without cash.
- Watch for drive-by bag snatchers when in parking lots or on sidewalks. Thieves also steal packages, especially from high-end stores and pharmacies (drugs).

- Do not wear your shoulder bag across your chest, because you could be grabbed and dragged. If someone wants your handbag, think, How important is it?
- Do not load up on packages; keep one hand free. Use packages, handbag, umbrella, or keys as weapons. Make more than one trip to the car, if necessary.
- Do not use headphones when walking or jogging. Be aware.
- Carry a whistle or electronic siren on your key chain. Be wary of sprays for self-defense. They may blow into your face.
- Carrying a gun or knife only assures that there will be a weapon on the scene—and it may be used against *you*.

TRAVELING

- *Never* take a ride with someone you do not know. Ever.
- If you use public transportation, use well-lit stops.
- Sit near the bus driver or the exit door.
- Never doze off on public transportation.
- Call ahead for a taxi (from a well-known company). Do not take one off the street.
- Match the taxi driver with the pictured license. Record the number. If there is no license in the taxi, get out.
- Do not drive with a taxi driver who seems in any way strange (high, tired, agitated, etc.). Pay attention to your instincts. At any time during the ride, if you feel discomfort, tell the driver to pull over and let you out.
- Exit the taxi close to your home, but do not identify where you live. Give driver your neighbor's address if you feel it is best.
- Only ride in cars that are in good condition, and have seat belts. Wear your seat belt!
- Sit in the back seat of a taxi, with your cell phone ready.
- Do not get into a taxi with another passenger you do not know.

BANKING

* Be aware of your surroundings before, during, and after bank/ ATM use.
* Have your ATM card readily available as you approach the ATM location. Block any view of your transaction.
* Place withdrawn cash securely on your person.
* If you see you are being followed after you leave an ATM, go to a well-populated, well-lit place. Call the police.

CATCALLING

Most females experience catcalling, or street harassment, at some time in their life, if not often. It usually comes as a whistle, honk, or comment while you are simply minding your own business. These experiences can range from a minor annoyance to a real threat, depending on the circumstances, but in any case, it often leaves girls feeling disgusted, offended, and scared.

As with any potentially threatening situation, responding appropriately is crucial. You must assess the situation to be sure you do not escalate the danger. You can choose to ignore it if you feel that is best. Some choose to confront it calmly and firmly, asking the offender why he would do such a thing, letting him know how they feel about his actions and that it is not okay, or asking how he would feel if this happened to his daughter. As always, be smart about it. You would not want it to turn into a more dangerous situation.

A MAN EXPOSING HIMSELF

When a man exposes himself to you, he is committing a crime. It's also another situation that can elicit disgust, fear, and anger for the victim. You need to respond to this in a cautious manner, because you don't know what this offender's intentions are, and you do not want to escalate this situation. First, you need to leave the situation immediately. Get to a safe place. You then need to report it to the police. Try to remember as many details as you can (hair color, height, age, the location and time of offense, etc.). Often these offenders repeat this pattern with other victims, and reporting him may prevent others from experiencing this crime.

ABOVE AND BEYOND

1. Just how far is thirty feet? We often underestimate this distance and reduce our ability to respond.
2. Which street safety guidelines do you already practice in your life?
3. Which three street safety guidelines will you implement in your life this week? Continue to add these to your life until you practice them all.

CHAPTER 9
Car Safety

• • •

Driving home from a concert late one night, I noticed a car riding alongside me. Since there were few cars on the road, I felt uneasy. I slowed down a bit to put some space between us, but they slowed down too. I sped up, and they sped up. I couldn't imagine why someone would do this. Was he trying to run me off the road? Was this a carjacking? How many people were in the car? Did he (or they) have a weapon? I tried to get away, but he would not allow it.

Not wanting to be isolated with him, I continued on the highway until the next busy crossroad, when I suddenly decelerated and exited the highway. Unfortunately, this person followed. I was several miles from a police station, hospital, or any populated building where I could find safety when I had to stop for a red light. As I slowly inched up to the other car, I looked over to see a man staring back at me and masturbating.

Disgusted and enraged, I followed this creep until I got his license plate number, which I reported to the police. Although nothing ever came of the incident, I still have this guy's face and car etched into my memory, as if it happened yesterday.

• • •

WHEN YOU TURN FIFTEEN OR sixteen, you are allowed to drive. You go to the department of motor vehicles, get a driver's manual, and study for the test. Yes! You pass with flying colors! Or you squeeze through by the skin of your teeth! Either way, you are now a driver.

So, with Mom or Dad, a driving instructor, or anyone brave enough to get in the car with you, you learn the rules of the road. Eventually, you set out on your own with proper driving skills, and you are good to go. But wait—there's one more important piece. Let us look at driver's safety.

CAR-ACCIDENT PROCEDURES

If you get into an accident, you must immediately stop. Unless you feel threatened by pulling over at that spot, you must stop and check all parties for injuries. If anyone needs medical attention, call 911. Then you should call the police, especially if the accident is serious or a hit-and-run. You then should exchange information (name, phone number, address, driver's license and plate number, and insurance details) with the other driver. Take pictures of the cars, if you can, and document all damages. Have all parties sign that documented information. If you hit a parked car and there is nobody around, leave a note with the appropriate information.

DRIVING TABOOS

- Neglecting to use a seat belt
- Being under the influence of alcohol
- Being under the influence of medication or illegal drugs
- Speaking on your phone for any length of time

- Texting
- Horsing around
- Applying makeup
- Playing really loud music .

Intentional "Accidents"

As you examine the car safety guidelines below, remember that while accidents do happen—yes, the kind where one person accidently hits another—intentional offenses also strike millions of people a year. By practicing the following safety precautions, you can prevent some of these terrible situations from happening to you. So again, study them, know them, and practice them.

Car Safety Guidelines

Before Leaving:

- Be sure you are in good physical condition to drive: well rested, able to move properly, wearing eyeglasses if needed, and *sober.*
- Prepare carefully for trips (check oil, gas, tire pressure) so that your car is in good condition. Know how to reach your destination. Use a GPS. Carry your license, registration, and insurance card. Have a flashlight in your vehicle.
- Check your gas gauge before each trip. Keep enough gas in your car (at least half a tank) so that you won't run out and become stranded.
- Never leave an extra key on the exterior of your car. Tape an unmarked spare key inside your bag.
- *Do not* put your name or address on your key chain.
- Don't put your name on a vanity plate.

APPROACHING VEHICLE:

* Make sure you are not being followed to your car. If you are, go to a safe and populated place, if possible, and get help. Set off your car alarm.
* Have your keys ready for a quick entry when approaching your car. Check underneath for someone hiding below.
* Look inside your car before entering (front and back areas, floors).
* If you return to your car and find it disabled (flat tire, dead battery, etc.), call someone right away. If you feel uncomfortable, leave immediately. Do not linger or accept help from a stranger. Who knows how your car became disabled?

PARKING:

* Park in well-lit areas. Be sure the lights won't go out before you return.
* Avoid parking next to vans, trucks, fences, shrubs, or anything that can obstruct your view or provide a hiding place for a potential assailant.
* Do not leave your house key with the keys that you give a parking attendant. Your address is easily obtained (from documents inside car, license plate, etc.).
* When leaving your car, lock all the doors and windows.
* Lock car doors as soon as you enter. If someone tries to enter your car while you are in it, lean on the horn, flash the lights, and make your car as visible as possible to encourage the threatening person to leave. If your car is running, accelerate and leave immediately.
* If someone enters your car and tells you to drive, consider bumping into another car at a stop sign or light. You may also hit a stationary car or fence on the passenger side. Be ready to release your seat belt and run.

In Motion:

- Wear your seat belt.
- Travel on well-lit and well-traveled streets.
- Keep car windows rolled up in unfamiliar areas.
- Do not take shortcuts through unfamiliar areas.
- When traveling alone, avoid stopping at night, if possible.
- Do not stop at rest stops at night or those with few cars even during the day.
- When stopped at lights or stop signs, leave enough space between your car and the car in front of you so that you can at least see the bottom of their back tires. This gives you enough room to go around them and leave the situation if necessary.
- *Do not* pick up people you do not know—even women, girls, or kids.
- If someone is driving you off the road or following you, drive to a public place like a police station, hospital, or firehouse. If need be, drive onto someone's lawn, honking your horn.
- Purchase or make a banner for the back window that says "CALL POLICE". Use it if your car breaks down. Turn on your emergency flashers, raise the hood, and tie a white cloth on the antenna or handle. Stay in your car with the doors locked. Ask anyone who stops to help you to call the police for you.
- If your car is hit from the rear, drive to a well-lighted, populated place before getting out to assess the damage.
- Do not stop to help a stranger in a stalled vehicle. Report it to police.

Above and Beyond

1. Which car safety guidelines do you already practice?

2. Which three car safety guidelines will you use in your life this week? Continue to implement additional safety tips.
3. Have a complete vehicle checkup to be sure your car is in good, safe condition: tires, battery, lights, oil, locks, gas, and so on.

CHAPTER 10
Dating Someone New

• • •

It was a group of us hanging out in the schoolyard on a Saturday afternoon. I had seen Phil around, and he seemed nice. So when we started flirting and he asked me to take a walk, I did. We went into the nearby woods, where he started kissing me and touching my body. I was scared and wanted him to stop, but I couldn't speak. I had no voice. I, who always spoke my mind, couldn't tell him to stop.

When it was over, we walked back and resumed hanging with our friends. I felt violated and ashamed. I wish I could have told him no.

• • •

BEING IN A CLOSE RELATIONSHIP can be one of the most fun and rewarding aspects of growing up. It feels so great to share time with someone you really like, to grab a slice of pizza, go out dancing, to a baseball game, or movie. Being close with someone has many rewards but can also present many challenges. Even though people of all ages have difficulties with relationships, teens often face more challenges because of the intensity of their emotions and the lack of experience needed to get through the rough spots.

Today, as kids are beginning to date as early as their tween years, most know of a friend who is involved in an abusive relationship by the time they reach high school. Dating violence is when one person tries to maintain power and control over another through abuse. The abuse can be physical, verbal, mental, emotional, financial, or sexual. It can happen at any age, regardless of gender, race, religion, or ethnicity.

As you begin dating, it is important to follow precautions and safety tips that will help to ensure you have the best possible experience, without putting yourself at risk for any danger. You want to be sure you know who it is you are opening yourself up to and to take things slowly so that you are aware of any red flags that might signal that this may not be the person for you.

DATING SAFETY GUIDELINES

* Only go on dates with people you know and trust. Get to know them on the phone or through group activities as much as possible before you meet one on one. Group dates ensure more safety, and your friends can offer feedback!
* Be careful about online dating. Do not meet an online date alone the first time. Bring a friend, and let others know the plan.
* Do a background check on the person. A simple Internet search will give you all kinds of interesting information.
* TMI—be careful not to offer too much information to someone you hardly know (address, financial info, etc.). Take it slowly, and develop a trust in the person before you give him something you can never take back.
* Be sure your family and friends know your plans: who, where, what, and when to expect you home. Tell them the phone number and other basic information about your date.
* Be prepared for the unexpected. Bring money and your cell phone with you.
* Pick a safe and secret place where a friend or family member can pick you up should you choose to leave.

- Know your values, personal boundaries, and limitations. Express these with your date. Be honest about what makes you feel comfortable and uncomfortable. A respectful, decent date will honor you and your boundaries. If your date tries to pressure you in any way to cross your boundaries, leave. Also, remember to honor your date's boundaries as well!
- Meet in public places. Remember, you do not want to be isolated with someone you really don't know. Do not go back to your date's place, or yours, at the end of the date. Use your own car or cab, or get yourself a ride to and from the date.
- Do not go on a date with someone who is drinking or using drugs. People drinking or using drugs are more likely to be reckless and violent.
- Alcohol and drugs will alter your judgment and increase your vulnerability. A drunk girl takes risks she wouldn't normally take and cannot take care of herself. Ideally, stay sober. If you choose to use a substance, be sure to have a friend look out for you, helping to keep you safe.
- Do not accept a drink from a stranger. Hold on to your drink at all times so that it cannot be tampered with. Date-rape drugs are commonly and easily used to make a girl unable to protect herself against sexual assault.
- Have a code word that your friends will know as your signal that you feel uncomfortable and need help.
- You have the right to refuse to have sexual contact, regardless of what you have said or done in the past and regardless of whether your date just paid for your dinner or gave you a diamond ring. When it comes to touching your body, your consent is needed each and every time.
- Trust your gut. If at any time or for any reason you feel uncomfortable, immediately leave. Call a friend and tell her or him you are coming home, or have your friend meet you where you are. Do not be alone with someone you feel uncomfortable with.

ABOVE AND BEYOND

1. If you are with someone and you become uncomfortable, what is your plan?
2. Who are your emergency contacts?
3. What is your code word to let someone know you need help?

CHAPTER 11

Having a Good Relationship

• • •

Our relationship was rocky, but I hadn't had the courage to end it just yet. We were at a wedding reception when my partner left for quite a while, completely missing the dinner. When he returned, he was irate, yelling at me for not keeping his meal for him. Knowing his tirade would escalate as usual, I tried to sneak out before he exploded, but he realized I was leaving. He charged the car as I exited the parking lot, repeatedly punching the windshield and screaming for me to stop. Unfortunately, he followed me back to our house in a friend's car, where his abuse continued, until finally he exploded out the door. It took another three months before I made a clean break from the relationship.

• • •

So what is a good relationship, and how do you know if you are in one? To some this may seem like a silly question. Of course you would know if you were in a good or bad relationship, right? Well, what you might consider "good" may not be very healthy for you. Most unhealthy relationships don't seem to start out that way. The dysfunction creeps in slowly.

Looking back, many people in unhealthy relationships report that they did see warning signs right from the beginning. Perhaps their instincts told them that a boundary was crossed or a harsh comment was made. Often people do know that something is wrong, but either they can't seem to place it, or they think things will change. The bottom line is that it doesn't matter so much if your relationship was at one point "good," what matters is what it's like now. Do not make a decision to do something or accept behavior that makes you uncomfortable out of fear of losing the relationship.

Many people in unhealthy relationships report that they did see warning signs right from the beginning.

A HEALTHY RELATIONSHIP

A healthy relationship is based on understanding, respect, trust, and open expression. Each individual has the freedom to have outside interests and relationships, to set boundaries that are good for him or her, and to come and go as he or she pleases. Each person has a right to his or her own thoughts, feelings, and needs.

AN UNHEALTHY RELATIONSHIP

On the other hand, unhealthy relationships involve jealousy, disrespect, threats, and violence. They are based on fear, manipulation, and control. Even if the relationship was at one time fun and caring, if it begins to feel restrictive, controlling, and frightening, it is *not* a healthy relationship.

BEHAVIORS IN UNHEALTHY AND ABUSIVE RELATIONSHIPS

- Threats (verbal or physical)
- Name-calling
- Constant criticism

- Jealous behavior
- Displays of temper
- Preventing contact with friends or family
- Destroying personal property
- Intimidating or manipulating
- Hitting, slapping, kicking, biting, shoving, choking, or punching
- Preventing you from going where you want, with whom you want, when you want
- Forcing you sexually
- Embarrassing you in front of others
- Stalking (repeated or unwanted contact, harassment, or threats)
- Mind games or teasing
- Manipulating you to spend money

Unhealthy relationships take many forms and affect every age, race, gender, and educational or economic status. It does not matter if you are young or old, rich or poor, or if the abuse is constant, sporadic, or a daily occurrence.

Any unhealthy behavior exhibited in a relationship is a warning sign. Take it seriously! Relationship abuse can be verbal, emotional, mental, financial, physical, and sexual. It can be between friends, girlfriends, boyfriends, parents and children, children and teachers, and so on. The intention is for one individual to maintain power and control over another. No matter what you have said or done to upset someone, you never deserve to be treated with disrespect. If you ever feel unsafe in any way, tell your parents, teachers, friends, counselors, or the police.

Even if these behaviors seem minor, they need to be taken seriously. Aside from the fact that they demean, control, intimidate, and hurt, these behaviors can progress to more violent treatment, like physical battering and murder.

Healthy relationships are life-giving, nurturing, respectful, and supportive. Even when emotions like anger, jealousy, hurt, or fear arise, as they do in all relationships, partners in healthy relationships do not behave abusively toward each other. Each person is free to express his or her feelings without fear of punishment. Each person is allowed to proceed however he or she believes is right for himself or herself. If one person decides to set a clear boundary, even if it means ending the relationship completely, the other must respect that boundary.

Victims of an abusive relationship show many warning signs, some more obvious than others. Whatever the type of abuse, many of these indications of abuse will appear no matter how hard the victim tries to hide it.

WARNING SIGNS OF VICTIMS IN UNHEALTHY (ABUSIVE) RELATIONSHIPS

- Changes in their eating and sleeping habits
- Avoidance of and isolation from family and friends
- Falling grades
- Dropping out of activities
- Loss of self-confidence; difficulty making decisions
- Tendency to be easily startled
- Sudden changes in mood or personality
- Increased risky behaviors (alcohol or drug use, sexual behavior, unhealthy weight control)
- Obsession with the dating partner
- Sudden changes in clothes or makeup
- Unseasonal dressing (e.g., long sleeves in hot weather to hide bruises)
- Scratches, bruises, or other injuries, especially in hidden areas (legs, torso, stomach, or head)

* Hearing loss (from strikes to the ears or head)
* Suicidal thoughts or behaviors

If you notice that a friend shows any of these signs, you must speak up. Do not let the abuse or the victim continue in silence. Ask them what is happening. Let them know they are not alone. Walk with them through this difficult time.

SPOTTING AN ABUSER

Abusers come in all shapes and sizes. There is no profile that fits all abusers, but there are some characteristics and warning signs that can send up red flags for you to take caution and move forward wisely. Abuser Red Flags include:

* History of childhood aggression
* Inability to take responsibility for their actions
* Substance abuse
* Poor self-image
* Prior arrest record
* Mental health problems
* Possessiveness
* Tendency to constantly give you gifts
* Constant calling or surprise visits
* Jealousy

GETTING HELP GETTING OUT

If you are in an unhealthy or abusive relationship, and especially if you notice any of these red flags in your life, you need to get help. Unfortunately, most victims are reluctant to tell anyone of their situation, and instead they live in isolation, fear, and continued abuse. Some may not even consider it abuse.

Often it is difficult for the victim to reach out for help, and she may instead minimize the abuse, feel guilty for leaving her partner, feel afraid of further abuses, feel shame or embarrassment, want to avoid getting her partner in trouble, or just hope that things will change. But, sadly, they will only get worse.

Across the country, there are many agencies available to help individuals who are involved in dating, domestic, and relationship violence. Look in your phone book or online for local emergency numbers, and you will find one of these support agencies. Write it down here:

LOCAL VIOLENCE HOTLINE #: (____) _____
National Domestic Violence Hotline #: 1-800-799-SAFE (or 7233)

Great. The next step is to call. Remember, relationship violence will get worse, so the sooner you make your first move toward safety, the better. When you do speak with someone, start by telling him or her what is happening in your life or how you feel. The other person will be able to help you go from there.

How to Ask for Help and Help Yourself (Now!)

* Tell someone about your situation. Call the hotline. Report the abuse to a school counselor, safety personnel, a parent or friend.
* Get professional help (counseling or legal assistance).
* Do not be alone with the abuser.
* Avoid being alone at school, work, walking home, and so on.
* Keep a log of the abuse (it will help if you need to get an order of protection).
* Make sure at least one person knows where you are supposed to be at all times. In case something goes wrong, he or she can call for help.

- Think about possible escape routes in case you need them (windows, fire escapes, etc.).
- Develop a safety plan for leaving, and rehearse it. Where will you go? What will you need to bring with you? What is the best time to leave?
- Choose a safe place to go (family, friend, or shelter).
- Pack a survival kit (money, some clothes, important documents, keys, prescriptions, valuables), and hide it in a safe, accessible place.
- Open your own bank account if you don't already have one.
- Avoid arguments with the abuser, especially in isolated areas or where potential weapons can be used.

Again, if you need help, call your local support system to assist you in this difficult process. These amazing people are there to help you. They will give you information on the various resources available for you, as well as your legal rights. Remember, you cannot change the abuser, but you can change how he will affect your life.

BULLYING

Bullying is unwanted, aggressive behavior that involves a real or perceived power imbalance. The behavior is repeated, or it has the potential to be repeated, over time. Bullying can take place in the school, on the bus, in the workplace, on the street—basically anywhere. It includes spreading rumors, excluding someone from a group on purpose, making threats, and attacking someone verbally, physically, or online.

Being bullied can be devastating and can have long-lasting consequences. But as with any hurtful treatment, there are effective behaviors and responses that can help to prevent, end, or lessen the effects of bullying.

Having an awareness of these various forms of bullying can raise your awareness of its prevalence. It may seem normal or harmless to tease or gossip. You know, "kids will be kids." But so often, the one on the receiving end of bullying behavior is hurt and scared, and often this behavior escalates. The first step is to know what bullying looks like and, further, to ask yourself if any of these behaviors affect you as a victim, witness, or offender:

- Leaving someone out on purpose; shunning
- Telling others not to be friends with someone
- Spreading rumors about someone; gossiping
- Embarrassing someone in public
- Hurting someone's reputation or relationships
- Name-calling, teasing, taunting
- Making inappropriate sexual comments
- Making mean or rude hand gestures
- Taking or breaking someone's things
- Threatening physical harm
- Hitting, kicking, pinching, spitting, tripping, pushing
- Damaging a person's possessions

Do these actions sound familiar? Are you a victim of these behaviors? Do you see others being bullied? Are you the bully? If you witness bullying, do you say something, or do you passively allow it to continue? It takes a lot of courage to stand up to a bully. If you see it happen and stay silent, you could be part of the problem.

Whether you are a victim of or a witness to bullying, you must face it quickly and directly to increase the chance it will end. As a witness, you may say something on the spot to support the victim, or you may tell an adult who can get involved. If it is happening to you, you need to know it is not your fault. However, there are solutions you can apply to your situation that can help. In dealing with bullying, as with any other dangerous and harmful situation discussed here, keep in mind that other interventions in this book can apply to bullying as well.

Wherever you go, if you project an image of assertive confidence, others will be less likely to bother you. Whether in the school hallway, on the sidewalk, in a boardroom, or in the bathroom, when you project confidence, awareness, respect, and calm, you are less likely to be considered a target by an offender.

Also, when you treat others with respect, kindness, and positivity, you may expect others to reflect that back to you. Even if you are targeted by an abuser, your first response should be a calm, assertive, and respectful one, so as not to intensify the situation. Remember, your goal is always to escape to safety.

Verbal bullying is a good example of an opportunity to diffuse a potentially dangerous situation. If someone says hurtful things to you, teases, taunts, and calls you names, how can you respond in a way that will minimize the damage? First, you need to know yourself and believe in your value. What others say is irrelevant when you have a strong belief in your value. If you let the words slide off your back and simply walk away, you prevent the bully from getting any power over you. Again, maintain awareness at all times, just in case.

Sometimes the situation requires more action on your part. As you assess the situation and determine whether more of a response is necessary, you must know your options and match the threat with a proper response. You do not want to overreact and intensify the situation, but you must protect yourself just the same.

Setting a clear boundary with your voice and your body is important when facing a bully. As with any assailant, he or she needs to know you will not allow yourself to be abused. Stand up to the bully in defensive mode with your palms up and shout, "No!" or "Leave me alone!" Yell for help if you feel you need help! Let bullies know that you do not want any trouble and that they need to leave you alone. Do this loudly and clearly so that anyone around becomes aware that this is happening. Remember, bullies do not want to get caught. Be firm and assertive.

If you are a victim of or a witness to bullying behavior, you need to tell someone—your parents, teacher, boss, supervisor, or the police. Depending on the scenario, you need to get help in ending the bullying as soon as possible, especially if it continues. Using your voice to the bully and asking for help will empower you and possibly end the offenses.

If the bullying is physical (pushing, hitting, tripping, any physical contact you do not consent to), you must promptly deal with it. Loudly and assertively telling bullies to stop is important, but sometimes it is not enough. What if you cannot just walk away? What if it escalates, and you believe you must respond with a physical defense? What options are available to you?

In all situations, physical self-defense should be a last resort. Responding with a kick or punch may send the message that you are serious about defending yourself, but it also brings you into a more serious predicament, one that you may not win. You may also suffer consequences for this response, finding yourself identified as the assailant, no matter how justified you may believe it to be. Schools and workplaces have no-tolerance policies that could put you in serious trouble. Also, especially if you believe the bully can physically overpower you, you will want to try everything else first. That said, when defending yourself, sometimes you will need to step it up.

In the age of computers, cyberbullying is a common form of bullying. This is the use of digital technology with an intent to offend, humiliate, threaten, harass, or abuse someone. As with any offense, it can be devastating, especially due to the speed that word gets around.

If you are a victim of cyberbullying, you want to let someone know. You do not need to deal with this alone. Take a screenshot or somehow copy the offense, and show it to someone who will listen and help you deal with it. Do not respond. This can escalate the problem and may even get you in trouble.

Just as with physical bullying, you will want to set boundaries. Online, you can block the bully and report it to the social-media platform you are using. This may be the end of it. If you feel threatened in any way, report it to your parent, teacher, supervisor, or the police. Like any bullying, cyberbullying is a serious matter that needs to be dealt with seriously and quickly. People do and say things online that they may not do or say face to face. People are not always who they say they are. You must protect yourself and be careful about inviting people into your world, even online (See Chapter 13 for Online Safety).

STALKING IS NOT ROMANTIC

We all like to feel flattered by the attention of a secret admirer. Knowing that someone thinks we are special feels good, right? Well, it feels good unless it doesn't, as in the case of a stalker. Stalking is a pattern of unwanted attention, harassment, or any other contact that would cause a person to feel threatened.

A stalker will use a variety of ways to monitor and have contact with his victim. The stalker so desperately wants a relationship with you that he does not care if it's positive or negative. Stalkers do not get the message that their attention is unwanted, or they dismiss, ignore, and disregard it. They do not care about your boundaries.

Stalking behaviors include the following:

- Making unwanted phone calls to the victim.
- Sending unwanted or unsolicited letters or e-mail.

- Following or spying on the victim.
- Showing up or waiting at places where the victim is (school, work, and home).
- Leaving unwanted items for the victim (gifts).
- Posting information or spreading rumors about the victim on the Internet, in a public place, or verbally.
- Making direct or indirect threats to the victim or the victim's family, friends, pets, or property.
- Obtaining personal information by accessing public records, Internet searches, going through the victim's garbage, following the victim, or contacting the victim's family or friends.

Stalking can happen to anyone. However, the National Institute of Justice surveys show that over three million cases of stalking happen per year and that females between the ages of eighteen and twenty-four experience the highest rates of stalking.

Most cases of stalking begin benignly. Victims often have a personal relationship, either romantic or platonic, with their stalker before this behavior even begins. That is what makes females believe they can handle it. But if you are a victim of stalking, you need to take it seriously. The National Violence Against Women survey shows that almost half of female stalking victims reported being directly threatened by their stalkers—many threatened with a weapon. Protect yourself, and get assistance to end this pattern.

This attention is repeated, unwanted, intrusive, and frightening.

CYBERSTALKING

With over three billion people with access to the Internet, it is no surprise that stalking behavior has traveled into cyberspace. Some stalkers find their victims on the Internet, while others use it to send e-mails, harass, or spread rumors on social media, chat rooms, and bulletin-board systems. This is a serious crime that calls for law enforcement involvement. (See chapter 13 on online safety.)

STRATEGIES TO END STALKING

- Maintain your safety (police station, family's home, friend, shelters), especially if you are in imminent danger.
- Contact 911, police, victim services, or a mental health professional.
- Get a restraining order (although this is no guarantee of safety).
- Utilize antistalking laws, and press charges through the local prosecutor's office.
- Document all incidents, including phone, text, or e-mail messages, witness accounts, and so on.

ABOVE AND BEYOND

1. Describe the characteristics of three healthy relationships you are in at the present time (e.g., fun, supportive, etc.).
2. Review the lists of warning signs for unhealthy relationships, victims in unhealthy relationships, and stalking. Do you see yourself in any of these pictures at the present or in the past? Explain.
3. If someone believes he or she is in a troubled relationship with *anyone*, what are the steps to safety? Write a plan as if you were in this situation. If you are, commit to your plan.

CHAPTER 12

You Always Have the Right to Say No

• • •

It was my twentieth birthday. We went out to celebrate. We were college sophomores, living in a city-based dormitory, blocks from several bars. I recall having drinks with two men we had never met. The next thing I remember is coming to in a bed, naked, talking with one of those men as he got dressed. I didn't know who he was, where I was, or how I had gotten there. And although I was completely horrified, my shame and fear led me to pretend as if everything were fine. Never missed a beat.

After dressing myself, I went into a strange living room, where my roommate sat talking with the two men. Again, as if nothing were wrong. He drove us back to campus and said he was getting married that day. "Congratulations," I cheerfully responded, although inside I was horrified.

I still do not fully remember what happened that night, nor was it ever discussed. On the inside, my deep sense of shame lasted years, and when I think about what did happen and what could have happened, I shudder.

• • •

Sexual Assault

Sexual assault includes any nonconsensual sexual contact or attempted sexual contact with a person of any age, race, gender, or sexual orientation. The offender may be—and usually is—a person known to the victim, or the offender may be a complete stranger. This crime is not about sex. It is about power, control, and violence. It is never the victim's fault, regardless of how she looks or dresses, or what the relationship was in the past. Here's the bottom line: if you say no to *any* sexual contact, for any reason, and another person pushes his will on you, it is a sexual assault.

Nonconsensual sexual contact is a crime.

- If it is a boyfriend, girlfriend, or a legally married spouse, and it is nonconsensual, it is a crime.
- If a person is unable to consent due to a medical condition or the use of alcohol or drugs, it is nonconsensual and a crime.
- If a person's will is overcome by force or by fear resulting from the threat of force, it is nonconsensual and a crime.
- If the person is in any way unable to communicate consent, it is nonconsensual and a crime.
- Silence is not consent.

Going through a sexual assault is a horrific experience that nobody deserves. The sense of fear and shame victims feel often interferes with their reaching out for help, and instead they bury themselves in anger, shame, fear, and depression. Victims need to immediately seek safety and help. You do not have to be alone.

There are people who are specially trained to help sexual-assault victims. If you or someone you know has experienced a sexual assault, you should go to the nearest hospital, where you can be treated by a trained sexual-assault nurse and certified crisis counselor. They will help you with your physical, emotional, and legal needs, including reporting the crime to the authorities. If you choose *not* to report it, you should still get help to heal physically and emotionally.

Resisting an attacker is only one of many options for a woman. Fighting back happens in many different ways—sometimes after an assault. Some women see reporting an attack to the police as fighting back.

It is never a victim's fault if she's sexually assaulted or raped.

REPORTING A SEXUAL ASSAULT

This can be very difficult, adding to the trauma a victim has already experienced. When you go to the hospital for medical help, you will have the opportunity to report this in a safe environment. They will not automatically call the police, as they must have your consent before doing so. They will, however, be there to assist you through it all. Even if you decide not to report it, they will collect any data needed to report, should you change your mind in the future. Reporting sexual assault not only helps you process the trauma but also helps police identify the assailant(s) and hopefully prevent others from being victimized.

If you are sexually assaulted:

* Call for help.
* Go to a safe place.
* Get proper and immediate medical attention.
* Do not wash or change clothes before calling or going for help.
* Do not touch any evidence of struggle.
* Ask a friend to stay with you.

To report or not report? *Silence is an assailant's best friend.*

Above and Beyond

1. What does "consensual" mean?
2. When is it a victim's fault?
3. If you or a friend is a victim of any sexual assault, what will you do?

CHAPTER 13

Online Safety

• • •

IN ORDER TO STAY SAFE in our world, we often focus on how to keep the "bad guy" physically away from us. We emphasize looking in all directions at least thirty feet away and listening for any approaching danger. These defensive measures require you to use all your senses, including your gut and your mind. It requires you to understand the situation in front of you and judge what your next move should be, based on the information you have.

But with Internet devices and relationships, you don't have all the information. You don't have all the facts, and what may appear to be true may very well be hogwash. You don't have the luxury of using your eyes, ears, nose, and even gut, since the person isn't in front of you.

When you enter the Internet world, new problems and challenges arise. These can often lead to mistakes you may regret for the rest of your life. These mistakes can come in the form of embarrassing personal information made public, or they can lead you right back into real-world, old-fashioned danger.

The contact you have with another person online can give you a false sense of security. It can also lower your inhibitions and give you a sense of false bravado. This can lead you to make poor decisions regarding safeguarding your personal information and personal safety. You might feel safe sharing an intimate thought or photo—or even your address. You may think you know this person well enough from the online world to meet him in the real one.

The information you share and post (address, phone numbers, school and work schedules, pictures, favorite hangouts) can be viewed by anyone (peers, teachers, colleagues, employers, ex-partners, thieves, predators, sex offenders, pornographers).

On the Internet, people can say whatever they want, and you do not have any way of knowing what is true. If a person pretends to be your age or someone with similar interests as you, there is really no way of knowing whether that's true.

Online, you do not have any control over who receives your information and what they can or cannot do with it. Online, there is no "take back" button. Once it's out there, it's out there to stay. So what you share with someone today can haunt you for the rest of your days. We have all heard about the e-mail or text message that went viral—or a lost job or college opportunity because of a Facebook account. This is why it is imperative that, if you decide to meet an online acquaintance in person, you *(1) never go alone; (2) meet in a public place; and (3) tell someone, preferably an adult, about the meeting.*

Other dangers that have multiplied as a result of the Internet are bullying, stalking, and sexual assault.

It is great to stay connected with your friends, but you must always remember that the information you share and post (address, phone numbers, school and work schedules, pictures, favorite hangouts) can be viewed by anyone (peers, teachers, colleagues, employers, ex-partners, thieves, predators, sex offenders, pornographers). Yes, predators may use your information. And don't forget, grandmas go on the Internet too, so be careful what you post.

SOME CYBER STATISTICS

* Up to 52 percent of teens know someone who has been involved in cyberbullying behaviors, including posting mean, hurtful, harassing, or embarrassing information or pictures; spreading rumors; publicizing private communications; sending anonymous e-mails; or cyberpranking (Harris Interactive-McAfee 2010).
* Over 75 percent of reports of sextortion (a form of sexual exploitation in which a child is threatened by nonphysical forms

of coercion, such as blackmail or humiliation, to acquire sexual content (photos/videos) of a child, obtain money from them, or engage in sex with them) involved female children. (The National Center for Missing and Exploited Children 2017).

* In a survey conducted by the Intelligence Group, the NBC news program *Dateline* questioned five hundred teenagers across the country about their computer habits. Fifty-eight percent said someone they'd met online had asked them to meet in person, and 29 percent said they had a "scary" experience online (Dateline NBC 2006).

CYBERBULLYING

We have all heard of incidences of bullying that either started on the Internet or were aggravated by it—rumors spread, fights recorded, even death threats publicized for all to see. Cyberbullying—whether through chat rooms, e-mails, or texting—is a crime. And, just like bullying in person, cyberbullying can cause a lot of trouble for both the victim and the offender.

If you are a victim of cyberbullying, tell someone. Don't minimize it just because your physical well-being may seem fine. It's not. The chance of this escalating into something beyond your control is great, so you must treat it as the crime that it is.

If you are involved in cyberbullying, even as a "bystander," you must report it. If it is on your computer, you are accountable. Remember, everything can be traced. If you receive inappropriate information, you are accountable. This includes any inappropriate pictures, even of yourself. And if the pictures are of an underage person, it is child pornography, which is a crime.

Sexting is when someone sends naked photos to others via cell phone or other devices. In one recent national poll, 20 percent of students say they have done it. We have covered why you should be leery of posting personal information or intimate photos of yourself online to people you only know through the online world. But you should be just as leery of sending explicit messages or illicit photographs via mobile phone or tablet, messaging, or e-mail to people you know in the real world, even boyfriends, girlfriends, or good friends.

Just like information you post online, information sent via e-mail or text can be easily distributed schoolwide, nationwide, or even worldwide in a matter of moments. No victim thinks she is going to break up with a boyfriend and watch the person she once trusted most in the world become a vicious adversary. But you need only look to the most recent bad breakup of a friend to recognize the possibility is there. So do not send any ammunition to a person who may one day be very hurt or angry with you. And if your boyfriend or girlfriend insists, then he or she can't or won't respect your boundaries, and it is time to move on.

Many schools across the United States have highlighted cases of sexting that had tragic results (e.g., Jessica Logan, whose experience with this led to her death). This is a very serious issue, and just as with our physical safety, there are many cybersecurity tips we need to use to stay safe in this global community of Internet users.

ONLINE SAFETY GUIDELINES

- Be a responsible, safe, good-mannered, law-abiding cybercitizen.
- Use updated antivirus software and firewalls.
- Do not click links on e-mail or download pictures from unknown sources, especially any e-mails that ask for sensitive information.
- Do not arrange to meet someone you've met online without letting others know your plans.
- Never upload pictures of yourself to others you do not know.
- Use hard-to-guess passwords, and keep them private.

* Do not share access to your computer with strangers.
* Use suitable filtering software to prevent exposure to inappropriate material.
* Limit what you put out there; do not give out identifying information like your name, home address, school, and so on.
* Use appropriate screen names.
* Do not possess or pass along inappropriate material.
* Do not engage in sexting.
* Do not engage in inflammatory e-mails, chats, and so on that are harmful to others.
* People are not always what they seem.
* Time does not equal trust.

Again, know that the information you share may someday come back to haunt you. There is no such thing as privacy online. Be careful to protect yourself against all these dangers just as you would against burglary, rape, and murder.

ABOVE AND BEYOND

1. List all the electronic devices you use and the number of hours per day you are connected to them. How many hours of the day are you asleep (and *not* connected)? How would you feel if you had to cut your connected time in half? Notice how much time you spend "alone." Notice how much electronic chaos is in your life.
2. Describe how these connections put you at risk for various dangers.
3. Using the online safety guidelines list, how will you protect yourself?

CHAPTER 14

Workplace Safety

• • •

He was mysterious and intriguing, and I was especially captivated by his adventures "on the road." Unfortunately, I ignored my better judgment and my friends' advice. Within days he moved into my small place and constantly showed up at my job. He even stole money from my tip collection, although he denied ever taking it.

Even when my workplace was robbed, and the police suspected my "boyfriend's" involvement, I still couldn't see it. I just couldn't. Until one night, he came home in a drunken stupor. I lay there frozen, as if asleep, while he literally bounced off the walls, rummaged through cabinets, and even urinated in the laundry basket. I was horrified. As soon as it was safe to leave, I grabbed my essentials and left town. I finally realized the dangers, and I wanted out, which I thought I'd made clear by leaving. About a week later, when he began showing up at my new job, I needed assistance in getting safely to my car at the end of each day. Security repeatedly asked him to leave, but he refused. I did all I could to block any contact, and eventually he was gone. I found out he was a convicted burglar who had spent many years in federal prison, and he was still looking for a life of crime and a willing accomplice in me.

• • •

ANOTHER HIGHLIGHT OF GROWING UP is financial responsibility. As you begin to stand on your own, you will have certain expenses, like housing, transportation, groceries, and clothes. Depending on your circumstances, you may even have to pay for healthcare and utility bills. The good news is how high your self-esteem will soar as you become fully independent and self-sufficient.

Okay, so maybe it's not all that; maybe it's not a highlight but simply a paycheck—a way to pay your bills and support yourself. Either way, we all need money, and a j-o-b satisfies that need.

Most people hold several jobs before they decide what it is that they want to be when they grow up. Regardless of what you do to make money, the workplace will always include a level of risk. When we practice the safety guidelines previously mentioned in *Taking Flight For Girls Going Places*, we already improve our chances of avoiding workplace dangers. Practices like expanding your awareness and trusting your gut will help you in all your endeavors. But there are particular guidelines to bring to the job that will further enhance your safety.

According to many labor organizations, certain jobs are considered more risky than others. For obvious reasons, these riskier jobs include mining, construction, law enforcement, and firefighting. But what about those positions you might hold that seem less dangerous, like waiting tables or working in a small shop?

The National Institute for Occupational Safety and Health identified the following factors that may increase workplace risk:

- Contact with the public
- Exchange of money
- Delivery of passengers, goods, or services
- Working alone or in small numbers

- Working late-night or early-morning hours
- Working in high-crime areas

Considering the risk conditions listed above, add to the list of risky workplaces gas stations, liquor and convenience stores, and drinking/eating establishments. When you think about it, any time you deal with people or are out in society, there is a risk. So really, to some extent, every job is a potential hazard.

What are the dangers we are talking about? Some of those dangers are inherent to the job, like a firefighter getting burned. But here are other conditions that put you at risk of becoming a victim of a crime or employer negligence:

- Environmental hazards (chemicals, pesticides, electricity, noise)
- Medical emergencies (burns, cuts, disfigurement, slips, disease)
- Physical safety (driving accidents, falls)
- Sexual harassment
- Drug and alcohol abuse
- Unsafe working conditions and practices
- Natural disasters
- Workplace violence (threats, verbal abuse, physical assaults, bomb threats, homicide)

To identify potentially dangerous situations in the workplace, it's best to use the safety precautions you would use anywhere else you may go. You need to always be aware of your surroundings, trust your gut, and act quickly on your own behalf. Additionally, here is a list of red flags for potential workplace violence:

- Inappropriate or aggressive behavior of coworkers, customers, or management (threatening, bullying, harassing, stalking, etc.)
- People with relationship, financial, or medical stressors
- Employees who often have conflicts with others

- Inappropriate statements regarding sexual harassment, violence, or firearms, especially workplace-related comments
- Substance abuse

If you have any of these concerns, use your best judgment to promote safety. Ask yourself these questions: Do I need to report it to a supervisor? Do the police need to be involved? In the face of workplace violence, an immediate, appropriate response is key. And remember, *you* must take responsibility for *your* safety. Don't wait for your boss, coworker, or company to make your workplace safe. It is in your hands.

So what will you do for money? How are you to choose a career when every option holds its own set of risks? What job *do* you hold, and how does it measure up in safety? Just as in all areas of life, the more we practice safety precautions, the safer we will be in general. You must incorporate workplace safety precautions into your job so that you can reinforce your security, increase your sense of power and productivity, and really enjoy the fruits of your labor.

The point is to take full responsibility for your safety wherever you go.

As in *any* situation, if you feel uncomfortable at your job, you must trust your gut, quickly assess the situation, and act appropriately. If that means you must leave, then leave. Better safe than sorry. At the least, *speak up*. Do not disregard your internal warnings just because you think you're in a safe place, even if you never had a problem there in the past. Trouble can happen even in the "safest" of places with the "finest" of people.

Here is a list of workplace safety precautions you can apply to your job. Remember, the point is to take full responsibility for your safety wherever you go.

WORKPLACE SAFETY GUIDELINES

SAFETY BEGINS WITH YOU:

- Be aware of your environment at all times.
- Trust your instincts.
- Treat all employees, customers, and managers with fairness, dignity, and respect.
- Be responsible for securing your own workplace.
- Do not work in risky places, if possible.
- Do not be alone, especially at night.
- Know safe places to escape to, inside and outside of the workplace.
- Be sure the building, parking lots, grounds, and surrounding areas are safe.
- Be aware of and report any verbal or physical threats or disruptive behavior. Take all threats seriously.
- Do not confront threatening individuals. Report them to management.
- Refuse to work if you feel unsafe. Report to a supervisor, a parent, or even the police if you feel threatened or endangered.
- Beware of coworkers who seem to be stressed out (marital, relationship, financial, or legal issues), who are loners or alienated, or who harass, bully, threaten, or are inappropriate in any way.
- Report suspicious persons or activities.
- Have zero tolerance for workplace violence (any bullying, defiance of management, sexual harassment).
- Work only for employers who have zero tolerance for workplace violence.
- Learn to recognize, avoid, and defuse potentially violent situations.
- Do not use drugs or alcohol at work.

- Report others who are using substances; they could endanger everyone there.
- If you work on the road, be sure to prepare daily work plans, and keep in constant contact with your office.
- Be sure your work vehicle is in good working order and properly maintained.
- Avoid traveling alone in unfamiliar places.
- Carry a minimal amount of money and identification.
- Be sure exit doors to premises are accessible. Alert your employer if necessary.
- Be sure the cash register is in clear view of the outside.
- Keep the cash register closed when not in use.
- Do not count money in front of customers.
- Keep doors locked (especially back doors when not in use).
- Leave with other employees; use the buddy system.

SAFETY IS THE BEST POLICY:

- Know and follow your company's safety precautions, policies, and procedures as directed by your employer.
- Know your workplace's history of health or other incidents (injuries, harassment, robberies, assaults, firearm use).
- Be involved in establishing, enforcing, or improving workplace safety.
- Get training for any health and safety issues (machine use, tasks, hazardous chemicals, etc.).
- Use appropriate protective gear and equipment (goggles, helmet, gloves, apron, footwear, mask, etc.).
- Report any hazards to your boss. If necessary, you can file a complaint with your company, your state labor department, or the US Occupational Safety and Health Administration.

* Post emergency-phone numbers near the phones for quick reference in case of an emergency or crisis.
* Document any incidents.
* Be sure the premises have security measures in place (silent alarms, cameras, money safe, door detectors, mirrors, panic button, bulletproof enclosures).
* Have a violence-prevention program in place.
* Post "Limited Cash on Premises" signs to deter robberies.

IN CASE OF AN INCIDENT, CRISIS, OR EMERGENCY:

* Know and use all emergency escape procedures and routes.
* Get any medical treatment needed.
* Call authorities (supervisor, police, fire, etc.).
* Secure the premises (leave the building if appropriate; lock up the building).
* Report and document the incident.
* Get appropriate follow-up treatment (medical treatment, counseling).
* If you have concerns about any situation, immediately tell your supervisor, and follow emergency procedures.

Whether you are in a part-time position or a lifetime career, you have a right to a safe and healthy workplace. It is your employer's responsibility to provide an environment that protects workers from injuries and threats, but ultimately you must determine if you feel safe in your workplace.

Do your homework before accepting a position. Be aware of any unsafe conditions. Follow all safety rules, and wear all safety equipment. Refrain from alcohol and drug use. Ask questions, and report any safety issues. Know your rights. After all, it is *you* who will suffer the consequences of job-related risks.

ABOVE AND BEYOND

1. What are the physical and environmental risks and hazards at your workplace?
2. What are your workplace safety precautions, policies, and procedures as directed by your employer?
3. What is the crisis plan or emergency plan at your workplace?

CHAPTER 15

Principles of Self-Defense

• • •

Working as a street vendor, I met all kinds of interesting people. One day, a very charming and fascinating man, made my day fly by as he talked of his escapades in horse racing. Once my shift ended, I agreed to go with him to dinner, where we drank a lot and talked about his adventures. We also discussed my life, and with little effort, he got me to reveal all sorts of personal information, including my phone number and home address. Throughout the meal, he persisted in inviting me to his place, but I wanted to finish my meal. Eventually, this stranger left the table and never returned. Later that night, after I somehow found my way back to my apartment, the phone rang. To my horror, it was him. The angry bite in his voice was chilling. He asked if I was "safe at home." Then he hung up. Thank God his patience ran out before my luck did.

• • •

OKAY, SO YOU HAVE TAKEN all the steps possible to prevent becoming a victim. You have put away the cell phone, opened your eyes and ears, and become more aware of your environment. Your new outlook on the various safety precautions, warning signs, or red flags is making a big difference in your life, and hopefully you have what you will need to keep yourself safe.

But let's go a step further—better safe than sorry. Imagine you do run into a situation where you must defend yourself. Imagine your boundaries are crossed, and your life is at risk. As you know, crimes happen even to those who take precautions. Sometimes we are powerless over what comes our way. The question is this: What will you do to meet that challenge?

The possibility of some type of offense happening to you is real. Remember, one out of three females become the victim of some type of assault in their lives. These victims did not ask for it. They were not at fault. But even with all the knowledge in the world, sometimes it's not enough to ward off a danger, so you must learn the many ways to proceed in the face of a danger to minimize risks and the consequences. Even if you know everything in the previous chapters—all the precautions and red flags—you are still at a disadvantage in an actual assault, because in defending your life, knowledge is key: knowledge of vulnerable body areas, effective defensive moves, and how to minimize incoming strikes.

Knowledge is key.

As we go further on the road to safety, keep in mind all we've discussed so far. Know that your ability to read a situation and respond appropriately depends on an awareness of your environment, people, and situations. The more you know, the better you can choose a defensive strategy.

CONNECTIONS BETWEEN KNOWLEDGE AND SAFETY

Knowing the mind-set of an assailant helps you devise a response. Knowing that assailants do not want to get caught and will look for victims they think will not give them a problem arms you with a defense. You will want them to know (1) you will *not* be a silent victim, and (2) you *will* give them a problem! Through assertive body language, using your voice, and other physical stances you choose, you will appear to be a poor choice.

If you believe you can de-escalate a potentially dangerous situation or prevent being harmed by staying calm, then you must trust your gut and remain calm. If and when you choose to strike back, don't hold anything back.

Knowing the effects of alcohol and drugs on a person can help you in your defense against someone who is drunk or high. You know that his balance is probably off, so you might strike his knees or shins to knock him to the ground—and then run to safety. You know you can expect sudden, irrational behavior. You also know he may be more interested in getting money than in hurting you, so you might decide to simply give him what he wants (your purse, jewelry, etc.) and hope he goes away.

In assessing a situation, you need to determine what the person is asking from you, what his state of mind is, what the chances of his getting more violent are, and what the chances of your overcoming these variables are. You must be able to read a situation using all your senses, including your instincts. And you must know how you will respond.

ABILITY TO RESPOND

For every threatening situation, there are many responses to choose from. This chapter will introduce various defensive options and help you process a mental and physical response. Let's walk through two scenarios and look at appropriate, safe courses of action.

Scenario 1:
You are in a club, and you accidently knock into Tom, who is obviously drunk. He becomes instantly agitated and begins to shout at you.

Scenario 2:
You are walking down the street, and Bob grabs your arm and tries to drag you into his vehicle.

In both of these scenarios, you need to be open to your gut instinct and mentally able to assess the degree of threat involved—that is, how dangerous the situation is. Then you must decide how to respond, based on the following general options:

* Escape
* De-escalate
* Comply
* Assert yourself
* Fight back

Each response holds a level of risk but will hopefully lead to your safe escape.

It is always best to start with the least amount of confrontation possible. You may only need to apologize nicely and walk away. In the case of Tom, the drunk guy in the club, fighting back is probably an overreaction. There is a good chance you can get away with a less risky response, like de-escalating the situation (by apologizing), and escape by walking away.

The case of the arm grabber is another story. Due to the aggressive nature of his approach, I would guess that a request to let go of your arm would be ineffective. Although a quick response is important, it will probably have to be more assertive and less nice! Let's go down the list of responses and see what might be the most appropriate for these two situations.

RESPONSES TO RISK AND DANGER
Escape: This is always the goal—to safely walk away from Tom or break free from Bob's grip.

De-escalate the situation: This could work with Tom as a next resort. You can apologize, sit down, even offer to buy him a drink (nonalcoholic, preferably) if that would avoid further confrontation. Bob, on the other hand, may be looking to hurt you, so de-escalating is probably not going to happen. If you can look strong and fierce, possibly discouraging him from pursuing his plan, great. But probably another, more aggressive level of response is needed.

Comply: This response will get you into Bob's vehicle and to a secondary crime scene. You definitely do *not* want to comply. If you thought Bob wanted your purse, giving it to him is an act of compliance that might save your life. Throw your bag in the opposite direction of your escape route and run. You have to figure out what it is the attacker wants!

Assert yourself: There are different degrees of assertiveness, from self-confident to firm to forward to "in your face." Knowing just how assertive you need to be takes an accurate reading of the person and situation.

Fight back: This response is the last option. You never want to fight if you can avoid it. In the case of Bob, the arm grabber, fighting back may be your one and only response.

*You must quickly read the situation, know your options,
determine the best response, and then put it into action!*

A note of caution: when using physical force, you should only use enough to protect yourself. If we go back to the club scene where drunken Tom is upset because you accidently bumped into him, you can try to de-escalate the situation first. If that doesn't work, then you will need to step up your defense.

Can you see the progression of aggression? You start out with the minimal amount of force that you think will fit the situation, and then you go from there. In that circumstance, you probably wouldn't immediately kick him in the knee or slam the side of his temple unless you believe the threat calls for it. Overreacting just might make the situation a lot worse.

Own Your Power!

You must own your power. What the heck does that mean? Okay, let's try a little centering exercise.

Center Yourself in Your Personal Power:

Sit quietly and relax your eyes. Imagine yourself in a warm, safe, and secure place. Think of all you have done to keep yourself well. Feel all the courage and wisdom you have within you as a result of all you know about yourself and about life. Think of all the people who love and support you. See them all there, smiling in honor of you. Think of your desire to freely engage in your life as you choose, your right to live without fear, and the freedom to be who you are meant to be. Imagine bathing in the power of this place, and then remind yourself it is all within you. Your power is within. Now, as you open your eyes, stand tall, and know you are strong, uninhibited, and ready to handle any situation that comes your way. You are in your true personal power.

Okay, back to reality. Don't forget to bring your personal power!

When you have assessed the situation as a threat and are beyond preventing an offense from happening, what do you do? First, you must remain calm. When you lose your bearings, you lose your power. Panic blocks positive action and induces a sense of powerlessness. So stay calm. You must focus on the situation and ground yourself in your power. Stand in the knowledge that you are strong, uninhibited, and ready to handle any situation you will face. And as you stand in those empowered shoes, *get mad!* That's right, *get mad!* Think about what is happening. *How dare someone take away your right to a safe, free, and happy life? How dare they?* Now, are you ready to defend yourself?

BASIC PRINCIPLES OF SELF-DEFENSE

* Never let yourself be taken to a secondary crime scene, a place where an assailant has more privacy to do what he wants. Stay in a public place where people can see you. Drop to the ground to keep from being pulled into isolation.
* Take advantage of the element of surprise. Assailants anticipate your reaction. When you make a decision to act, do not let the assailant know it is coming. Catch him off guard. And once you commit, don't hold back.
* Maximize your power. When you strike, be sure to use maximum body strength. Keep your balance, rotate your hips, execute a survival scream when striking, and give it your all.
* Use your strongest weapons against the assailant's weakest targets. Know your body and nonbody weapons. Know the vulnerable parts of his body to strike. Make your strikes count.
* Use a series of significant, effective defensive moves until you can escape to safety.
* Keep barriers between you and your assailant (doors locked, furniture, trees).
* Attract attention in any way you can. Scream, drop to the floor or ground, blow your car horn, flash your lights. Let the offender know you will *not* cooperate.
* If you feel threatened, act like you will defend yourself with a weapon by putting your hand in your pocket or handbag.
* If you are alone, go to where people are. Run, climb out a window, and so on.

Body Language

Attacks on females, whether sexual or not, are acts of violence. Offenders seek to demonstrate their power over potential victims, so they need someone who will offer little resistance. In choosing their victims, they usually watch several girls and pick one. How can you *not* be the one they pick? Appear confident, alert, and attentive in your body language and your voice. Stand tall and strong, chin up, and walk forward, showing that you are completely aware and confident in your journey. This body language will show a would-be attacker that with you, there *will* be resistance.

The Survival Look

Go over to a mirror and put on your meanest face. *Grrr!* Remember how mad you were when you imagined someone trying to take away your safety, freedom, and happiness. How *dare* they? Now look fierce, and let your face show your determination to fight for your life! This is the look you want a potential assailant to see.

Okay, so you have a great smile, and your eyes could charm the stripes off a tiger, but this is not the time to draw someone toward you. No, you want to repel him like the swine flu. You want an attacker to wish he had never caught sight of your beautiful face. You need to put away your happy face and *get ugly*.

Defensive Stance

Imagine that someone approaches you. He could be asking if you want to buy Girl Scout cookies or come for a ride with him to who knows where. How can you say no with your body? A simple gesture would be to lift up your palm to him and shake your head no. If the attacker approaches you, and you believe he is going to swing at you, step back with one foot, and put up both palms to block any incoming strikes.

That is a defensive stance. While this can simply mean "no thanks," it will also put you in a good position to block, strike with a powerful punch or kick, or run away.

THE SURVIVAL SCREAM

You know the scream, the one that comes from that deep place within yourself. The one that makes you jump back and wonder who the heck just did that! Like a tremendous power surge from within, it's that scream that will send the message that you are a *survivor*—not a victim.

When you get in touch with your *voice*, you will have no problem executing a survival scream. Try it. *"No!"* And again. How did it come out? Puny? Laughable? Passable? Solid? How about nonnegotiable? Listen: you need to find your voice. Your voice will communicate your truth to the world. It will help you set boundaries. If you do not have a strong connection with your voice, you will be overshadowed by the voice of others. This is the case on all fronts: friends, family, school, and job. You must be able to speak up for yourself, especially in the face of a threat. Is your voice committed to your safety and your goals? Is it honest, direct, and fearless?

Try it: "NO!" And again.

There are many benefits to having a strong, determined survival scream. First of all, when you assert yourself with a deep belly roar, you loosen yourself up and unblock your energy. This allows you to be more in a position to defend yourself—emotionally, mentally, and physically. Second, you let the assailant know that you are 100 percent committed to defending your life. If an assailant still wants to mess with you, he will know it won't be easy. Remember, assailants do not want to get caught. Hopefully, after he hears your scream, he will run in the other direction!

Your scream can also confuse the attacker and alert him that help is on the way. Shout out whatever gets the attention of others: "Fire!" or "Help me!" or "This man is attacking me!" or "Call the police!" or "@#$ &*!"—*whatever gets attention*. And if and when you do strike, be sure to yell your survival scream with all your might at the instant your strike hits the assailant. It's like directing all your energy toward the target for maximum power.

Last but certainly not least, do not worry about being polite. Save your manners for those who deserve them, and take care of yourself. Remember, honest, direct, and fearless. When it comes to self-defense, nice girls do not always win.

ABOVE AND BEYOND

1. Describe three threatening situations you have seen in your life. Using the information in this book so far, what would be the best responses to each?
2. Practice
   your body language;
   your survival look;
   your defensive stance; and
   your voice (survival scream).
3. Imagine walking down a dark street and being approached by a creepy someone. Go through the above moves to repel this person. Walk with proper body language, show your survival look, take a defensive stance, and let loose your survival scream.

CHAPTER 16

Offense and Defense

• • •

After biking at the beach, I returned to my car just before dusk. There were only a few other cars in the parking lot. As I put my bike onto the rack, I noticed a man approaching me, his pace unusually forceful and serious, and my gut told me he was looking for trouble.

I scanned the area for assistance and then turned to face him square in the eyes. I wanted him to know I was not going to be his prey. My heart pounded, and I thought I was doomed, but I knew I needed to stand strong and defend myself. I became really angry. How dare he!

Suddenly, as if he realized how much trouble I would give him, he abruptly turned around and left! I will never know what this man's intentions were that day, but I don't think he was there for a swim. I do believe had I not handled it with confidence and determination to not be a victim, the story might have had an unfortunate ending.

• • •

WHEN YOU COMMIT TO PROTECTING your physical body from the harm of an assault, you will do whatever it takes. Remember, you want to start out with the minimal amount of force that you think will fit the situation and go from there. That said, let's get down to the nuts and bolts of self-defense. All of these moves are simple, natural, and instinctive actions that basically anyone can do. This isn't karate. If you want to earn your white, yellow, green, orange, purple, brown, or black belt, then go to a martial arts studio. This is a practical, inexpensive, quick way to learn basic prevention and self-defense.

BLOCKING

You are innocently walking down the street and someone or something comes at you. You must respond, or you are going to get socked. The most sensible, most natural thing to do is move out of the way. Right? Just move out of the way.

Now say that doesn't quite work, for one reason or another, and you must deflect the strike. That is, you must cause it to sidetrack your body. When an object or a fist or a foot comes at you, it is best to let it continue in the direction it is naturally going. Think about catching a hardball without a mitt. That would hurt, right? You wouldn't want to catch it with a sudden slam into your palm. You would instead want it to ease into your palm as you slowly pulled it away in the direction it is moving.

Well, it's the same with blocking. If a punch is coming at you, instead of sticking your arm up like a wall and stopping it point blank, you would move your head to the side and use your forearm to ward off the strike away from your face. You simply push it away from your head, allowing it to continue in the direction it is going.

It's the same with a kick. If a foot is coming at you, rather than abruptly stopping its motion with your forearm, simply direct the foot away from your body using your forearm, allowing it to continue in the direction it is already going. It's much easier and less painful than blocking to a dead stop.

As your block directs a punch or kick to move past your body, the person who threw the punch or kick will probably spin so that his side or back is now to you. This gives you the chance to easily strike him or get away. So, to *deflect* with a block, you allow the person's movement to proceed naturally; allow it to go with the flow.

Most blocks call for you to use your arm as an instrument. To be most effective and avoid hurting yourself, it is important that you have proper form. A blocking arm should bend at about ninety degrees, depending on the position of the strike. Often it will start as a ninety-degree angle and then extend as you push away the strike. Blocking hand positions call for a strong, solid fist or a strong, solid chop. Either way, it should be a strong, firm form, with fingers in tight so that they aren't injured. This applies to striking hand positions as well. The chopped hand should be in a cupped position, so your fingers are slightly bent. This gives your hand more power.

There are several block positions that can be used in a variety of scenarios. Which one you will choose depends on where the strike is coming from. Obviously, a kick to your leg is much different from a punch to your face, so you will need to block differently. Will you use a high block, a midblock, or a low block? Naturally, you will want to block from the same area where a strike is coming. So you would use a high block to a strike coming at the head or upper body, a midblock for a middle-of-the-body strike, and a low block for a kick to the lower body. You still use the same principle of allowing it to go in the direction it wants to go. You just position your arm differently.

BLOCK AND STRIKE
The ideal scenario would be for you to block or deflect a strike coming at you and then escape to safety. Chances are, though, that you will need to

follow up with a strike to further disable the assailant. The following section gives you solid tools to do just that. Strike an assailant until you can escape to safety.

Remember, you want to use the appropriate amount of force that the offense calls for. You do not want to make matters worse, but you don't want to stop striking until you can escape, either. And don't forget to continue with various strikes to different parts of the body until you can escape to safety.

VULNERABLE PARTS OF THE BODY

This could be the most important defensive information to know. Read it, memorize it, practice it, and know it. For one, these are vulnerable parts of everyone's body, including your own, so by knowing this material, you will be in a better position to protect yourself. Second, the only way you will really make your strikes count is to hit the vulnerable parts of your offender's body. Strike 'em where it counts!

No matter how hard you strike, if you don't hit an assailant where it counts, you are wasting your time, your energy, and your chance of survival. If a two-hundred-pound monster is coming at you with the worst of intentions, and you hit him with all your might on his forearm or back, it's not going to matter much. In fact, you may actually make him angrier and more determined to conquer you. He may even laugh at your feeble attempt to defend yourself. Either way, it's not going to help your situation at all.

Throughout our body, there are many areas that are more likely to give way in the face of pressure. Whether a bone, joint, or nerve, these spots are great targets to aim for if you want to disable or harm a person. The list below gives you a full-body perspective of the areas you should aim for. Again, *know them.*

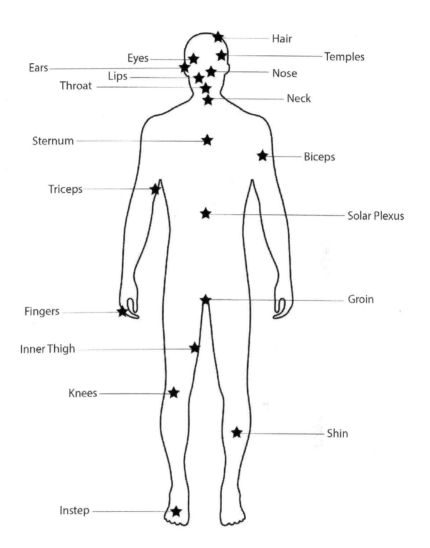

Vulnerable Body Parts

- **Eyes:** Poke, jab, spit, throw dirt, or spray with hair spray. Damaging his vision gives you the opportunity to run.
- **Temples:** Jab with your knuckles or an object for a dangerous blow.
- **Ears:** Slap with cupped hands, give a chop, or poke with fingers. These strikes can burst the eardrums, impairing his hearing and balance.
- **Hair:** Pulling hair can give you control over where his head will go (like into your knee).
- **Under nose/bridge of nose:** A strike here can cause eyes to water, impairing vision.
- **Lips:** Grab and twist; just be careful putting your fingers near his mouth (to avoid being bitten).
- **Throat:** A good strike to the throat can cause choking and death. Very dangerous.
- **Neck:** The side nerves or back where the spine joins the skull are very sensitive; raking with knuckles can cause much damage.
- **Sternum:** A hard kick or stomp to the center of the chest can break ribs and impair breathing. Also, raking the ribcage can cause him to release you.
- **Solar Plexus:** A jab here can knock the wind out of an attacker.
- **Biceps and triceps:** A tight pinch here hurts a lot!
- **Little finger:** Bend back, grab, and twist.
- **Groin:** A solid kick or punch can disable. Grab, twist, and pull testicles.
- **Inside of thigh:** A tight pinch here hurts (femoral nerve).
- **Knee:** A solid kick can disable.
- **Shin:** Kick or scrape with the edge of a shoe (or a book or other object).
- **Instep:** There are many nerves on top of the foot. Stomp.

You want to use your strongest weapons against his weakest targets.

In the face of an offender, you will quickly need to know which areas of the body you should target. As you get to know this body chart, physically and mentally practice the spots you will strike, if need be. You do not want to be in the position of needing this information and not have it. Learn this material now so that when you commit to striking, you automatically know what to do. Do not waste your time, your energy, or your strikes!

You will need to automatically know where you need to hit—or can hit—and take that opportunity to make your strike count. Whether you will strike with a fist, a foot, a cell phone, or a book, you will always want to make your strikes count by targeting one of these vulnerable areas. Remember, you want to use your strongest weapons against his weakest targets.

BODY WEAPONS

Again, you want to use your strongest weapon against your offender's weakest target—your strength against his weakness. So what are your weapons? Basically anything that can be used to distract, impair, or disable an assailant is a potential weapon. A train whistle can be a weapon if it temporarily distracts an attacker so that you can run to safety.

Just as the human body has many vulnerable areas, there are also strong points on your body that can be used as a weapon. Just your hand alone gives you the ability to block, chop, punch, scratch, rake, poke, jab, knuckle, throw, grab, twist, and pull! That is some weapon! Yes, your entire body is jam-packed with natural weapons at your disposal—whenever you need them, wherever you are. By arming yourself with this knowledge, you are arming yourself with these weapons.

Your number-one defensive *and* offensive body weapon is your brain. You will use it to know, avoid, and properly respond to every situation. Before engaging in an argument or physical altercation, you need to think about and understand what is happening. As discussed before, sometimes all that's needed to diffuse a situation and avoid an assault is a verbal response. You may be able to simply respond with calm, nonoffensive words and then safely leave. But first you need your brain to understand the situation in front of you and know which response is most appropriate.

Now, if the situation requires more defensive action, you will need to know an attacker's weak targets and your natural weapons to maximize your defense—that is, which strong body part is best to use against the offender's vulnerable areas.

STRONG BODY PARTS

- Brain (understand; know various and appropriate preventions and responses)
- Front and back of head (to strike the offender)
- Voice (talk; alert bystanders; make survival scream)
- Teeth (bite)
- Saliva (spit)
- Nails (scratch)
- Hands (hammer fist; vertical fist; back fist; ridge hand; palm heel; uppercut; hook shot; fingers to eyes; fingers to throat; fingers to grab, twist, and pull lips or groin; fingers to grasp and snap pinky; fist to box ears; finger poke; knuckle poke)
- Elbow (jab up, down, and to the side)
- Knees (strike offender in any area, especially head, abdomen, groin)
- Legs (front kick, side kick, back kick, roundhouse kick, knee strike, foot stomp, shin scrape with heel of shoe)

RANGE DEFENSE

When physically defending yourself, there are important defensive strategies to remember. First, as the danger comes at you, you must choose the proper move to deflect the attack. The distance from a danger will dictate which defensive move is most appropriate and effective. For example, if the person is ten feet away, you aren't going to rush into him with a punch to the temple when you can use other, longer-range weapons against him, such as your brain, voice, leg, or umbrella.

On the other hand, if the attacker has you in a bear hug, kicks to the groin probably will be ineffective, if not impossible. Realistically, you would need to use closer-range strikes, such as an elbow to the sternum, knee to the groin, or forehead to the nose. Again, you must know all your options so you can respond at a moment's notice.

DOMINO FIGHTING

If your first strike doesn't work to allow you to escape to safety, you will want to continue striking until you can get away. You will use a series of successive strikes, targeting the attacker's vulnerable spots until he gives up or you can get away. For example, you can use a knee to the groin, then a palm heel to the nose, then box the ears, then—you get the point. Keep your defensive strikes going, if necessary!

MAXIMIZE YOUR POWER

When you do strike, you want to be sure to pivot your hips and bend your knees to maximize the power and force of your strike. And don't forget to use your voice!

INSTANT WEAPONS

Along with body weapons, we often have items within our reach that we can use as a weapon. A perfect example is the cell phone. Most people don't go anywhere these days without a cell phone. In fact, it's rare to see a person walking, especially alone, without a phone actually attached to his or her head! So there's an instant weapon ready for your defense. How is a cell phone a weapon? First of all, you should have emergency numbers ready to dial with the touch of a button. You can also use a phone to strike the top of or underneath an assailant's nose—or his temple, throat, sternum, or groin. Got the picture?

Other weapons are listed below. The idea is to know the vulnerable body areas and use whatever is available to strike where it will count. As you read the list, decide how best you could use these weapons to defend yourself.

INSTANT WEAPONS CAN INCLUDE:

- Cell phone
- Rolled-up magazine
- Umbrella
- Flashlight
- Hair spray
- Brush or comb
- Coins
- Credit card
- Book
- Video box
- Package or shopping bag
- Handbag
- Pencils or pens
- Briefcase or book bag
- Sand or dirt
- Water bottle or soda can
- Any liquid in a cup or bottle

* Plastic bottle (sunscreen: squirt in the eyes or strike with the container itself)
* Shoes
* Keys

WEAPONS

Arming yourself with offensive and defensive tools can make the difference between preventing, avoiding, minimizing, or surviving danger. Knowing the safety guidelines, vulnerable parts of the body, and hold releases matters. Faced with any potential threat, you must be able to assess a situation and know what to do. And, as emphasized throughout *Taking Flight For Girls Going Places*, the number one weapon you possess which can make a difference is knowledge.

The numerous tools throughout this manual can prepare you to physically defend yourself if needed. The options are vast, the commitment essential, and some decisions more considerable than others. In deciding whether to own a weapon, you must know what options are available to you to decide the best course of action. Although having a weapon may increase your sense of security and safety, unless it is the right one for you, and you are well-instructed and practiced in its use, it could lead to more problems than it's worth. This decision is serious and should not be taken lightly.

Some of the available weapons include:

* An alarm system
* A dog
* Martial arts
* Keychain alarm
* High powered flashlight
* Pepper spray (Mace)

- Kubotan (pocket stick)
- Stun gun or taser
- Knife
- Firearm(gun)

Just as each weapon has particular benefits, so does it carry its own unique risks. Pepper spray can be ineffective in the wind, rendering you as the one disabled. A gun may be more effective in deterring or disabling an attacker, but the risks are high. Having a gun on the scene increases the chance that it will fall into the wrong hands - a child, suicidal person, or the attacker. Ultimately, having *any* weapon on the scene increases the risk that it will be used for unintended purposes, including against you.

If you consider getting a weapon, you must learn about all the risks involved. Do your research. You want to be certain it is safe and practical. You also must get full and proper instruction to insure maximal effectiveness and safety - thorough training is crucial! And, you need to check with your local and state laws to find out about any age requirements, necessary permits, and legality of each weapon.

Whatever line of offense or defense you choose, you must train yourself until employing it is second nature. To fully experience the benefits of any potentially lifesaving strategy, you must practice. The time to know *how* to use these tools is *before you need them*!

WEAPONS USED AGAINST YOU

What do you do when someone is threatening to use a weapon against you? Should you comply and do what they tell you to? Do you fight? And how do you know when to do what? There is no easy answer.

You will be the one who needs to read the situation, determine the threat level, and act accordingly. First, you need to know as much as possible about the situation in order to respond in the safest way. And even when you do have all the information, there still is no guarantee that things will turn out in your favor. You simply have to do the best you can with what you've got. So *what can you do now* so that you are armed with the knowledge when you need it? You are doing it by reading and knowing and practicing the information presented in *Taking Flight*.

Let's imagine that you are confronted with a weapon. Here are two scenarios:

Scenario 1: You are walking down a quiet street one night, and a man approaches you with a knife and demands your pocketbook.

Scenario 2: You are walking down a quiet street one night, and a man in a car stops, points a gun at you, and tells you to get in the car or he will shoot you.

This is the time to call to mind all the knowledge you have about safety, people, the environment, self-defense, and life in general. You are in serious danger, and your commitment to defend your life must be absolute.

Questions to Ask Yourself:

* What is being asked of me, and how important is it? My purse? Money? My car? My life?
* What does my gut tell me about the situation?
* What does it tell me about the offender?
* What could happen if I did what is asked of me? If I gave him my purse? If I got into the car?
* What is the status of the aggressor? Does he appear to be drunk or high?
* Do I have a history with this person? If so, how has he behaved in the past?

- What are my options?
- Could I try to diffuse the situation and avoid further trouble?
- Do I have the skills to protect myself against the weapon?
- Am I in a position to fight off the weapon?
- Is there a chance I could run to safety?
- Will getting into the car take me to a secondary crime scene? Will it be the last decision I ever make?
- Where can I run to safety?
- Is anyone else around to help me?
- How can I minimize the damage done?

Particularly when there is a weapon on the scene, you want to remain calm and in control. This is not the time to get hysterical, especially if the attacker is agitated, drunk, or high. If you decide to resist his demands and fight back, you want to wait for the right moment and then fully commit to your plan of defense. You will want to act with sudden, powerful moves. Up until that point, you want to speak slowly, keep eye contact with the attacker, and stay calm. And then, when it's time—*bam!*—you make your move. Then you want to scream and punch and kick those vulnerable areas of his body until you can escape to safety.

Generally, when fighting someone who has a weapon, you will want to gain control over the arm or hand that holds the weapon and then follow up with a strike. If you get possession of the weapon, use it to your advantage until you can escape to safety. This may mean shooting or stabbing your attacker in self-defense. This may sound crazy, but it may be the safest thing you can do. If you decide to run away from an armed attacker, you want to run in the direction of people and light, and run in zigzags, not a straight line. You also want to minimize the attacker's target (you) and crouch down or use things in the environment to block his aim.

There are many ways to fight off and disarm an attacker. If you want more advanced knowledge and skill in this area, find a personal trainer who can physically assist you in the specifics of the various circumstances and weapons.

HOLDS AND RELEASES

You are walking down the street, minding your own business, and someone grabs hold of your wrist in an attempt to control you. Or they come behind you and wrap a forearm around your neck in an attempt to strangle you. Can you believe it? *How dare they!* In this very dangerous situation, you will automatically have red-alert signals going off in your brain, because you know you are in big trouble, and the time to fight for your life is *now*.

Escaping from an assailant's hold can be tricky, especially if the assailant is physically bigger and more powerful than you. And although you must do whatever works to release yourself and escape, there are specific tactics you can learn to increase your chances of escape and survival. So what will you do? Well, getting angry is a good start.

When you are in someone's grasp, that person is in control. The attacker can do with you whatever he chooses unless you take back control. The attacker can throw you to the ground; drag you down an alley; and beat, rob, rape, or kill you. Or he can drag you into a vehicle that will take you to a secondary crime scene, and then he can do as he pleases. Your ability to free yourself from the attacker is crucial—and the sooner the better.

When you are ready to make the break from the attacker's hold, you need to fully commit to your plan of action. Your first move to release should be fast, unexpected, and *loud* in order to startle the attacker. And based on what you know about the situation at hand, you can decide to simultaneously strike him while releasing, or you can follow your release with a strike, being sure to target the vulnerable parts of the body to make your strikes count. Hopefully then you will be able to run to safety, but if not, you strike again. And you continue to strike where it will matter until you can get away.

When you are in someone's grasp, that person is in control. The attacker can do with you whatever he chooses unless you take back control.

Below is a list of holds and releases. As with the rest of the defensive moves in this book, it's important that you practice them until they are second nature. The time to learn them is now, not when you need them. Some of these releases are quite simple, and some are more complicated. Don't worry about fancy footwork. Get down the basics, and go from there.

HOLDS AND RELEASES

Wrist-Grab: If someone grabs hold of one or both of your wrists, your first response should be to hug your elbows close to your body so that you are not further injured (arm twisted or broken) or manipulated (dragged or pushed to the ground).

To understand the mechanics of a wrist release, grab your left wrist with your right hand. Notice that where your right fingers (thumb and forefinger) meet is the weakest area, the point at which you could most easily release your left wrist. That is the key to the wrist release. If you grab your left wrist from underneath, you would abruptly pull up with the left arm and simply release it. If you grab the top of your left wrist, abruptly push down with your left hand to release. Get the idea? Again, you want to use your strongest move (a sudden, unexpected pull) against the attacker's weakest area (where his fingers meet).

Usually, you are not holding yourself in a wrist grab, so you have your other hand to use in your defense. You can grab your held arm and use the force of both hands to push or pull toward the attacker's weakest area (where his fingers meet). You can also use your free hand to block any strikes coming at you or to strike the attacker, which can add to the shock and power of your defense. Remember, you can kick and scream as well.

You also can grab the attacker's thumb with your free hand, pulling and twisting it back so that you lead him toward the ground. Then you can strike or escape to safety.

Hand on Your Shoulder: If someone puts his hand on your shoulder in an attempt to push or pull you, you can spin that arm in a big circle forward and back toward his arm. Now you have the attacker's hand in a hold and can push or strike him—or escape.

Arms around Your Shoulders: In this type of high hold, you can lower your body, spin away, and move back—with a strike if needed. As you're in close range, you will be in a position to knee or punch the attacker's groin or knees. If he has your arms in the hold, raise your arms as you bend over and jab an elbow into his groin.

Low Bear Hug: When in a low bear hug, you need to use close-range moves to escape. You can raise your arms and elbow the attacker's sternum, rake his temples, or strike his vulnerable facial areas. Know what these vulnerable areas are—and the accompanying strikes to use.

Front Stranglehold: The stranglehold is one of the most dangerous positions. Because your air supply is cut off at the side of the neck or your windpipe, you have about ten seconds before you lose consciousness. In a front strangle or choke hold, you must get the attacker's hands free from your neck. Cross your forearms in front of you, and push the attacker's arms away. You can follow up with an elbow to the face or a knee to the groin, but you *must* release the attacker's hold on you.

Rear Stranglehold: Again, release the attacker's hold as quickly as possible. As you pull down on his arms with all your might, lower your chin to your chest, lower your body, and spin away from him. Be sure to block or deflect his strikes while you strike him or escape. Remember, releasing the attacker's grasp on your neck is your first concern.

On-the-Floor Straddle: When you are on the ground in any position, you are less able to get away. Especially if the person is on top, straddling you, you need to be committed to an aggressive response. First, you need to deflect any punches coming at you. You can also thrust your hands through the attacker's arms to jab his face, eyes, and throat. Here are two options: (1) In order to release from this position, put up your left knee and wrap your other leg around the attacker's ankle. Grab the attacker's shirt, and pull him toward you, and then turn your body over them so that you end up on top. Then strike vulnerable spots (punch nose, throat, etc.). (2) Put your heels together, lift your hips, and back up. Alternate lifting each side to throw the assailant off balance and off you. Continue with striking the attacker's vulnerable areas until you can escape to safety. Again, this is a dangerous position, so make your strikes count. The goal is to get up and away from the danger.

Defense from a Seated Position: If someone approaches you while you are in a seated position, the goal is to stand up soon as possible and move away. Whether in a movie theater or a classroom, if you become uncomfortable in any way, you should immediately stand up before the person gets too close, if possible.

Your strongest body weapons from a seated position are your legs. Unless the person is coming from behind, strong kicks at an attacker can keep him at a distance and hopefully give you the opportunity to get upright and away.

You can also use the defensive strategies suggested in the previous sections for the various holds. For example, any hold around your neck needs to be met with a quick release to assure your ability to breathe.

Lying Down (Bed, Beach, Etc.): Anytime you are on the ground, your goal is to get up and get away. Remember, the best defensive stance is to be standing upright with your arms blocking your torso and face, feet ready to kick or run, and voice projecting your commitment to defend yourself. If you are on the ground, you have little chance of escaping until you can get up.

From the ground you will want to use your legs to keep distance between you and the attacker and to strike vulnerable areas (knees, groin) to try to disable him. Be sure to protect your head from the attacker's kicks or strikes. You can sit on your butt, using your hands to swivel around as you kick. If you are outside, grab dirt, sand, gravel, or whatever is handy, and throw it hard into the attacker's face and eyes.

Continue to use whatever weapons may be at your disposal (shoes, rocks, sticks, etc.) until you can get up and away. If you are in your bed, use the clock, a book, the phone, or a lamp as your weapon. If needed, continue to strike once you are upright till you can escape.

The best defensive stance is to be upright with your arms up, feet ready to kick or run, and voice projecting your commitment to defend yourself.

Multiple Attackers: When there is more than one attacker, you do not want to become the monkey in the middle! You have a better chance of escaping to safety if you take on one offender at a time. If possible, you need to line yourself up so that you are constantly on the end—that is, not in between them—with no one behind you. This requires steady movement, but it is important. Once you are lined up, you can strike one attacker in his vulnerable areas to try to disable him. You can also try to push one into the other and get them both down so that you can run.

In choosing which attacker to approach first, you must decide which scenario would give you the best possible escape opportunity. You may choose to have the weaker attacker in the middle and use him as a buffer between you and the stronger one. Or you may choose to go for the stronger one to show that you are not afraid to do whatever you need to defend yourself.

This is not a good situation, no matter how you slice it, so it's important to try to keep yourself calm and know your plan. Remember, you do not want to fight two people at once if you can help it. Try not to have anyone behind you. Keep scrambling to keep your back safe, taking effective shots at the attackers when you can. It's a lot of fancy footwork, but for your benefit you must stay aware of where they are at all times.

Caution! The time to plan your response to a violation is *now*. Don't wait for it to happen and expect an automatic defense. Know what you will do. You must *practice, practice, practice!*

ABOVE AND BEYOND

1. Exercise: Pretend a potential attacker approaches you. You step back, put your hands up in a defensive stance, and yell, *"Stop!"* The attacker continues toward you. Deflect any strikes coming at you. Pick a vulnerable spot, and strike (punch, knee, kick, etc.) while yelling again. Continue striking vulnerable spots until you can *get away.* Name all of the vulnerable areas of the body you would target.
2. Practice blocking: high block, midblock, low block.

3. Name your body weapons and how you could use them.
4. Define "range fighting" and "domino fighting."
5. Name ten improvised weapons at your disposal right now.
6. Practice the following holds and releases: wrist grab, hands on your shoulders, arms around your shoulders, bear hug, front and back strangleholds, floor straddle.
7. How will you defend yourself from a seated position, on the ground, or if there are multiple attackers?

CHAPTER 17

Being Present to Yourself

• • •

The freedom to be my true self—that's what life is all about: to walk through each moment without fear or doubt about my ability to handle what will cross my path, to create a life that reflects to the world how awesome and loving and fun and compassionate and bright I really am.

I was born with a toolbox. As I go through life, I gather tools that I can use to live my life to the fullest. And while life is being life and "stuff happens," I have what I need to cope and grow. I have the skills and the supportive people I need to walk through life with self-respect and dignity.

I am grateful to my creator for this amazing life and for the opportunity to share my experience and strength with others so that they may be free to be their true selves.

• • •

So NOW WHAT? ARE YOU supposed to live in fear, suspicious of people everywhere you go, expecting the worst? How can you enjoy life when you're on guard? Well, the point of learning about various dangers and appropriate responses is certainly not to create a fearful you. The point is to heighten your awareness of the dangers out there, prevent them from crossing your path in the first place, and give you automatic defensive strategies that can help to minimize harm if you *do* face a threat.

"Yes, but now I'm paranoid," you say. Well, yes, unfortunately our society gives us reason to distrust and be on guard, and you need to be prepared for the worst. But the paranoia you may feel now will subside as you empower yourself with this material and become more confident in your ability to protect yourself.

Think about your experience in attending a new school. Those final days of summer were probably consumed with worry about getting lost in the strange hallways and being late to class. Think about those first-day-of-school jitters that you thought for sure everyone could read all over your face. But by day three, you leisurely walked through those same hallways as if they were your second home. You could actually stop at your locker, go to the restroom, catch up on the day's gossip, *and* make it to class before the bell rang! How in the world did you do that? *Practice.*

As you successfully handle new challenges in life, you will learn how competent you are, increase your self-esteem, and feel more confident to handle future challenges. This self-protection knowledge can increase your confidence and esteem, just like your knowledge about your new school gave you the confidence to navigate those hallways without worry or even thought.

Eventually, you will learn to incorporate the information into your thoughts and behaviors, and you won't have to think about all the horrors out there. You'll just live differently.

You will automatically consider safety first. You will ask yourself questions like these:

1. While going to the mall, for example: What time is it, and how long do I plan to be there? Will it be dark? Should I ask a friend to go with me? Where is the safest place to park? How will I get safely back to my car?
2. When walking home from school: What is the safest route? Am I alone? Is it dark?
3. When using a public restroom: Can it wait till I'm in a safer environment? Are there other people around, or will I be isolated?

In other words, you will *have a plan.* When you sit down in a movie theater, the first thing on the screen is what? Images of where the emergency exits are! Well, you need to do the same thing. Know the emergency exits and have a plan.

Obviously, not all situations raise the same level of threat, and in some cases, having an emergency plan may be overkill. Probably Grandma's house is safe enough that you can relax about your safety. But why not have a plan when you go to the movies or the mall, just in case? Why not practice the defensive moves, just in case?

VICTIMHOOD

Millions of women know that to be a victim of a crime is to be stripped of your sense of self. Even when you know it wasn't your fault, the subsequent fear, guilt, anger, and shame you feel will, at a minimum, block your connection to yourself. Ask yourself, "Who am I?" No matter what you would have answered before a victimization, your answer will have changed afterward. The chance of escaping any offense—especially a serious one—without repercussions is quite rare, if not impossible.

A victim's life is turned upside down. The consequences of crimes such as stalking, robbery, and sexual assault touch every area of your being: physical, mental, emotional, financial, and spiritual. You must give yourself the follow-up treatment necessary for healing, or you will live a lifetime of victim behavior. A victim who experiences a physical, emotional, or psychological trauma goes through several reactions.

Posttrauma Experience:

* Shock, disbelief, denial, numbness, confusion
* Anger, rage
* Guilt
* Depression, withdrawal
* Fear, terror of returning to work or school
* Fear of criticism from others
* Sense of powerlessness, helplessness
* Grief, sorrow, loss of sense of security

After an offense, victims need time to gain back trust, as well as their sense of control, balance, and self-confidence. They need to gain some understanding of the trauma, as well as its impact on themselves and others. There are several factors that will determine the impact an incident has on an individual, including the duration of the event, the lack of control she had over the event, the amount of injury or loss from the event, her previous victimizations, and her ability to handle stress.

Whether that person is you or someone you know, take advantage of the *many* healing supports available to move through the experience with more knowledge about yourself and the world around you. You do not have to live with the wounds from a crime. You are worth more than that.

A Note from the Author

Today, when I start to get a sense of an approaching threat, my instincts alert my mind, and I automatically upload what I have internalized. Like the files on my computer, it is instantly there for me. I think of the red flags and warning signs. I see in the offender all the vulnerable areas as if they are highlighted with neon lights. My body is programmed to respond in the best way possible. This is due to practice.

Fear can be your best friend—yes, fear. Not worry, but instinctual fear. Throughout this book, I shared with you several true experiences from my life in which I landed as a victim or potential victim. Although I was unaware of it at the time, many of these experiences came with pre-incident warning signs that could have saved me a lot of trouble. When I think back on each experience, I can see where my fear was trying to help me, but for one reason or another, I did not or could not listen.

Just like when we are about to leave the house and something tells us, "I am forgetting something," we are given that inner voice through-out the day. Do we listen? Well, I urge you to *listen to that voice*! It is the same voice that will keep you aware and protected. Like an alarm system in your home, that voice will alert you to important and possibly lifesaving information, and it can help you to live in more freedom and more safety.

ABOVE AND BEYOND
Personal-Responsibility Statement

Below is your place to create a personal-responsibility statement. This is your personal commitment to and specific plan for taking care of yourself.

1. What do you want for your life?
2. What are you willing to do to make that happen?
3. How will you prepare to take responsibility for your safety?
4. What changes will you make to assure a safe environment wher-ever you go?
5. How important is your safety?

RESOURCES

• • •

BELOW IS A LIST OF vital resources available to those in need. The time to prepare is now, not in the moment of crisis, when time is of the essence. Please add any other numbers or websites that could be useful in the future, whether to you or someone else. Again, it's better to be safe than sorry. Most of these resources can be found in your telephone book or on the Internet.

Fire:
Police:
Physician:
Dentist:
Counseling Center:
Suicide Hotline:
Local Hospital:
Campus Police:
Psychiatric Emergency:
Department of Social Services:
District Attorney, Victim Advocate:
Legal Aid Society:
Crime Stoppers:
Domestic Violence Hotline:
Alcoholics Anonymous:
Narcotics Anonymous:

ABOUT THE AUTHOR

• • •

KATHY GREENE LAHEY, LMSW, AC, has dedicated her career to empowering females. She is a licensed social worker, addictions counselor, activist, and blackbelt. She developed *Taking Flight* workshops, which give girls and young women the skills they need to grow and thrive.

Lahey herself is a survivor of sexual assault and other gender-based harassment. In *Taking Flight For Girls Going Places*, she focuses on prevention and arms independent-bound girls and young women with the information needed to feel comfortable, confident, and safe.

Lahey has three children and one granddaughter. She lives and writes in Port Jefferson, New York.

Website: www.girlsgoingplaces-us.com
Follow us on facebook: @girlsgoingplaces.us
Follow us on instagram: @girlsgoingplaces.us

REFERENCES

• • •

Abbey, Antonia. 2002. "Alcohol-Related Sexual Assault: A Common Problem among College Students." *Journal of Studies on Alcohol, Supplement 14*:118–28.

Association of American Universities. 2015. *AAU Climate Survey on Sexual Assault and Sexual Misconduct.* https://www.aau.edu/key-issues/aau-climate-survey-sexual-assault-and-sexual-misconduct-2015

Baum, Katrina, Shannan Catalano, and Michael Rand. 2009. *Stalking Victimization in the United States.* Bureau of Justice Statistics Special Report, Department of Justice's Office on Violence against Women. NCJ 224527.

Bureau of Justice Statistics. 2010. *National Crime Victimization Survey.* Department of Justice, Office of Justice Programs. NCJ 250180. https://www.bjs.gov.

Collins, J. J., and P. M. Messerschmidt. 1993. "Epidemiology of Alcohol-Related Violence." *Alcohol Health & Research World* 17:93–100.

Dateline NBC. 2006. "Most Teens Say They've Met Strangers Online." NBC News. Last modified April 27. http://www.nbcnews.com/id/12502825/ns/dateline_nbc/t/most-teens-say-theyve-met-strangers-online/

Fisher, Bonnie S., Francis T. Cullen, and Michael G. Turner. 2000. *The Sexual Victimization of College Women.* Research report, US Department of Justice, Office of Justice Programs. NCJ 182369.

Grunbaum, J. A., L. Kann, S. A. Kinchen, B. Williams, J. G. Ross, R. Lowry, and L. Kolbe. 2002. "Youth Risk Behavior Surveillance—United States, 2001." *Morbidity and Mortality Weekly Report* 51 (4): 1–62.

Harris Interactive-McAfee. 2010. "The Secret Online Lives of Teens." https://promos.mcafee.com/en-US/PDF/lives_of_teens.pdf

Magliano, Joe. 2015. "Why Are Teen Brains Designed for Risk-taking?" *Psychology Today,* June 9.

National Institute on Alcohol Abuse and Alcoholism (NIAAA). 2010. "Underage Drinking." https://pubs.niaaa.nih.gov/publications/under-agedrinking/Underage_Fact.pdf

National Institute of Justice and Centers for Disease Control and Prevention. 2015. *Full Report of the Prevalence, Incidence, and Consequences of Violence Against Women Survey.* US Department of Justice. NCJ 183781.

Planty, Michael, Lynn Langton, Christopher Krebs, Marcus Berzofsky, Hope Smiley-McDonald. 2013. *Female Victims of Sexual Violence (1994–2010).* Department of Justice, Office of Justice Programs, Bureau of Justice Statistics Special Report. NCJ 240655.

Sinozich, Sofi, and Lynn Langton. 2014. *U.S. Department of Justice, Bureau of Justice Statistics Special Report: Rape and Sexual Assault Victimization Among College-Age Females (1995–2013).* NCJ 248471.

The National Center for Missing and Exploited Children. 2017. http://www.missingkids.com/theissues/onlineexploitation/sextortion

Truman, Jennifer L., and Rachel E. Morgan. 2015. *Criminal Victimization, 2015.* U.S. Department of Justice; National Victimization Survey. NCJ 250180.

Vagi, Kevin J., Emily O'Malley Olsen, Kathleen C. Basile, and Alana M. Vivolo-Kantor. 2015. "Teen Dating Violence (Physical and Sexual) Among US High School Students: Findings from the 2013 National Youth Risk Behavior Survey." *JAMA Pediatrics* 169 (5): 474–82.

World Health Organization. *The United* Nations *Study on The Status of Women, Year 2000.* Department of Reproductive Health and Research, London School of Hygiene and Tropical Medicine, South African Medical Research Council. 2013.

Made in the USA
Columbia, SC
10 July 2018